Fig. 1 Collage of hand-knit swatches.

The Knitting Design Book

Using color, pattern and stitch to create your own unique sweaters.

Ank Bredewold   Anneke Pleiter

Lark Books
Asheville, North Carolina

Drawings: Anneke Pleiter, Hetty Paerl,
Amsterdam
Photography: Hans van Ommeren,
Woerden; Ank Bredewold, Amsterdam;
Peter Mitchell and Tom Smith, London, Fig. 9
Art design: Karel van Laar, De Bilt
Translation: Cornelia Tieken-Neal
for Net Works, Inc., Highland, Maryland

Cover photo courtesy of E'Lite Specialty Yarns, Inc.

Published in 1988 by Lark Books
50 College Street
Asheville, North Carolina, U.S.A. 28801

First published in the Netherlands under the title
Breien naar eigen ontwerp
© Uitgeverij Cantecleer bv, De Bilt 1985

Library of Congress
Cataloging-in-Publication Data
TT825.B7313   1987   746.9'2   87-36146
ISBN 0-937274-41-0

Printed by South Sea International Press Ltd.,
in Hong Kong

Please note that while we have exercised every care in the
compiling of these patterns, mistakes do sometimes occur,
and neither the author nor the publisher can accept any
responsibility for damage to materials or machines which
may occur, due to errors in printing.

CONTENTS

6

Fig. 2 A photo of a Picasso painting inspired the designer of this sweater

1. INTRODUCTION

In this book you will be introduced to designing your own original hand-knit garments by using a variety of methods.
The following subjects will be covered:
1. Where to get ideas for designs.
2. How to translate your idea into a working drawing.
3. How to adapt it for hand-knit garments.
In the various chapters of this book that deal with designing knitting patterns, different aspects are highlighted and suggestions are given for carrying them out.
To make a good design, technical knowledge of knitting is not a major factor.
Since knitted garments are stretchable, it is necessary only to have a simple, basic pattern. Simply make a paper pattern using your own measurements or use a well-fitting sweater. This is your basic tool for creating different sweaters, utilizing varied materials, stitches and colors.
The more time you give to designing your pattern, the better it wil be. You must knit gauge swatches to try different stitch variations. Do not consider this wasted time. It pays off in the finished product.
It is a very good idea to save your gauge swatches with a short description of how a particular idea developed and whether there were any technical problems in working it

out. You can always reuse these samples for future designs.

In this book you will not find elaborate patterns, just simple sweaters to use as examples when designing your own pattern.
The pictures shown on this page, for instance, show how a picture taken on your vacation can be turned into a sweater design.

3a   3b

7

Fig. 3 A wall of a mosque in Tunisia. The geometrical pattern on part of the wall was transferred onto graph paper (Fig. 3a). The motif is repeated in the design (Fig. 3b).

Fig. 4 This drawing shows a jacket in which the enlarged pattern was used randomly. Used sparingly, the motifs became very decorative ornaments.

2. DESIGNING

The designs in this book are mainly for sweaters. Of course, it is possible to apply the same ideas to other projects, such as jewelry.

Since it is not easy to just jot down a good design on a blank piece of paper, you will probably do better to start with:

1. a picture or a slide
2. the shape of a garment, or
3. stitches and yarn.

1. A picture in a book or magazine could become part of a knitting pattern. The picture, or even more interestingly, part of the picture, can be translated into a working drawing, using several different methods of approach.

2. The outline of a piece of clothing can be used, filling in the shape. This "filling-in" will be very different if the shape is round or square.

3. Fig. 7 shows yarn made of different materials. Using interesting materials can automatically lead to a design.

Starting a design from a picture
A picture, slide or drawing can inspire you to design clothing. You are probably familiar with sweaters which have comic strip characters or flowers embroidered on them.
In beginning your design from a picture, you could use the complete picture for your design. However, you can achieve a much more interesting design by using just a portion of that picture. Simply cut a piece of tracing paper into the shape

of a miniature sweater. Slide it over the picture you are using until you find an interesting fragment. Enlarge this fragment onto graph paper and you've got your design! You could also use a slide, projecting it onto a piece of paper cut into the shape of a sweater. Simply trace the portion of the slide onto the paper sweater with a pencil.

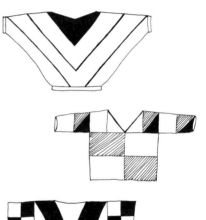

Fig. 6 Outlines of sweaters used for determining your design. If diagonal lines are used, such as a V-neck or raglan sleeves, these lines can be accentuated by a jacquard motif.
If you use rectangular motifs, the shape of the sweater can be adapted by using a boat-neck and straight sleeve lines.

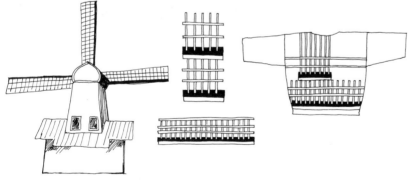

Fig. 5 Drawing of a windmill, used as a starting point for a design. You could use the entire windmill in your design if you wish. The sketch on the right shows that only certain details of the drawing have been enlarged, so that the original windmill cannot be identified as such. This procedure can make coming up with an idea for a design much easier.

8

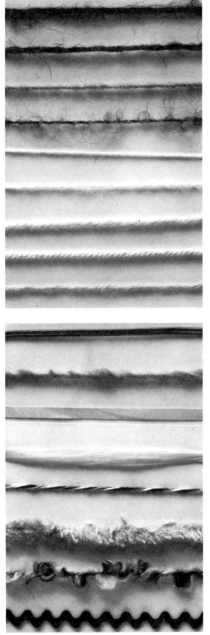

Fig. 8 Magazine photo of a clothesline.

Fig. 7 The diversity of yarns.

Fig. 8a. Slide a piece of tracing paper, cut in the shape of a sweater, over the picture until you find an interesting fragment for your design.

Fig. 9 Zebra skin was used for a design.

Fig. 10 Using a square frame, this interesting portion was chosen for the design.

Fig. 11 The motif was placed on graph paper by the designer.

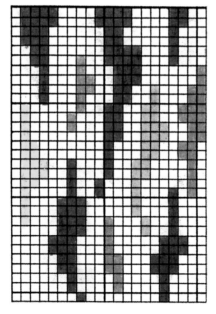

In Fig. 12, for example, a sweater is shown which used a picture of a zebra for the design. A square frame was used (Fig. 10) to find an interesting portion of the picture. This section was then enlarged onto graph paper. You may not find it very original to use an existing picture, but the originality lies in the fact that it is up to you to decide what part of the picture will be used, where you want to incorporate it in the sweater, which stitches you apply and whether you will maintain or vary the colors.

In the zebra sweater, the original black and white stripes are changed to yellow, orange, dark blue and light blue.

Starting a design from the shape of a garment.

The shape or outline of a garment can form the starting point of a design, which you complete by filling in the blank space.

You may develop an idea by draping a piece of fabric around your body. The shape the fabric takes can be used for your design. The original shape of the piece of fabric will naturally affect the outcome. For instance, a circular piece of fabric, folded asymmetrically, and draped around your shoulders, like a cape, may suggest using it as a double collar.

But, if you cut a neck opening in the center of the same piece of fabric, you will achieve a totally different effect. Extra fabric can be pleated or used for sleeves. Draping this circular piece of fabric may give you the idea for designing a sweater with a round collar.

A triangular piece of fabric draped

Fig. 12 The final result of the zebra design. Gauge: using size 4 needles: 4″ + 19 sts x 26 rows in St st.
Front and back: with size 3 needles, cast on 90 sts in dark blue and work 3″ in K1 P1 ribbing. Continue with size 4 needles and work in St st, increasing 20 sts evenly spaced across the first row. Knit the design following the graph. When work measures 17½″, shape sleeves by binding off at each edge of every second row: 6 sts 1 time, 5 sts 1 time. Continue to work on the remaining 88 sts until work measures 23½″.
To shape yoke and neckline work as follows: Find the center st and mark it with a different colored thread. In the first row work 2 sts in K1 P1 ribbing on each side of the center st. In every following row work 2 more sts in K1 P1 ribbing at each side of the center st, until all sts are worked in ribbing.

around your body can lead to an asymmetrical closure (Fig. 13). Experimenting with several triangular shaped pieces of fabric by overlapping them or connecting them in a certain way can create very interesting designs.
For the design shown on page 12, a square piece of fabric was used, with a smaller square cut in the center. The final result is shown in Fig. 17; this sweater was made on a knitting

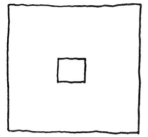
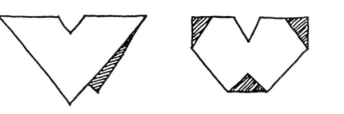

Fig. 13 A square piece of fabric, with a square opening cut in the center, was the beginning of a sweater design. When the outside is worked in a different color than the inside, decorative variations can be obtained by folding back the corners. The square piece of fabric can also be folded diagonally.

12 machine.

The idea for this design came from draping the fabric diagonally around the shoulders. The design could be changed further by folding back the corners of the fabric. In the finished sweater, the inside was knitted in a contrasting color; by folding the corners back the design takes on a different and interesting effect. Another idea would be to knit the sweater in one color and the folded triangles in another.

You could also knit a square by beginning at one corner and working diagonally by casting on one stitch at each edge on every 2nd row and making increases in every row until you reach the desired diagonal width. Then decrease on every 2nd row until one stitch remains.

Designing with stitches and yarn

Ideas for designing knitted garments can also be derived from the stitches

Fig. 14 Wall of a Tunisian building with bricks laid in a highly decorative pattern.

I knit   — purl

Fig. 15 Graph for knitted design in Fig. 16. Vertical lines represent knit stitches and horizontal lines represent purl stitches.

Fig. 16 The Tunisian wall was interpreted in the knitted garment by alternating knit and purl stitches.

Fig. 17 This poncho was made on a knitting machine. Stitches were cast on the total width of the knitting machine. The poncho is a square, with a square neck opening. It was knitted twice; the outside in green, the lining in gray. Portions of the poncho can be folded back, showing the inside, knitted in a different color.

and yarn you will be using. Swatches of different yarns in a variety of stitches can help determine your design.

You will see how the "walls" theme was used in structuring different designs.

The first example is a photo of a wall in a Tunisian town (Fig. 14). You can see the complicated pattern in which the bricks are laid. On the swatch in Fig. 16 and the graph of Fig. 15, the design of the pattern is imitated by alternating knit and purl stitches.

The second example is a sketch of an ordinary brick wall (Fig. 18). Here the design in the swatch (Fig. 19 and 20) was worked in berber yarn, mixed with traces of mohair strands.

By incorporating the mohair randomly, the "bricks" are given an airy effect of exposure to weather. Stitches used: knit and purl (see Fig. 20).

The third example is a stone wall

Fig. 18 Sketch of a brick wall.

Fig. 19 The brick wall motif in this sweater was worked in one color. A strand of mohair, incorporated randomly, was used to give the "bricks" a weathered effect.

I	I	I	—	—	—	—	—	—	—	—	—	—	—
I	I	I	—	—	—	—	—	—	—	—	—	—	—
I	I	I	—	—	—	—	—	—	—	—	—	—	—
I	I	I	I	I	I	I	I	I	I	I	I	—	—
I	I	I	I	I	I	I	I	I	I	I	I	—	—
I	I	I	I	I	I	I	I	I	I	I	I	—	—

Ⅰ knit ⊟ purl

Fig. 20 Graph of brick wall motif shown in Fig. 19.

(Fig. 21) which distinguishes itself from a brick wall by its rough and irregular surface. You can clearly see the hues of brown, beige, gray and green in the picture. To get that same effect, strands of different yarns have been used in the sweater. When using several different yarns, you do risk a chaotic look. To prevent this, and to achieve an overall unity, this sweater was worked in the woven barred stitch, using different colors of the same type of yarn.

Fig. 21 A stone wall.

14

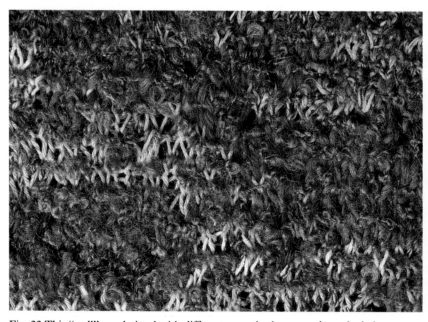

Fig. 22 This "wall" was knitted with different yarns in the woven barred stitch as follows. Row 1: K. Row 2: *K2, sl 2 purlwise*, repeat * to *, end with K1. Repeat these two rows.

3. BASIC KNITTING TECHNIQUES

Knitwear

All hand knitting begins with a number of loops being cast on to one needle; further rows are then worked into these loops. Knitwear is stretchable and is therefore extremely suitable for garments. Knitted fabrics (double knits) are very often used in sportswear. Knitwear is very fashionable today. Sweaters can be oversize, loose and casual and do not have the sole purpose of warmth, as was the case of densely knit fishermen's sweaters (Fig. 23).

The sweater in Fig. 24 was designed for the purpose of accentuating the outline of the body and was definitely not made for wearing comfort. Because knitwear is stretchable this could easily be accomplished, no zippers or buttons had to be used.

Another characteristic of knitwear is that it can be raised in relief from the surface (how much, of course, depends on the stitches used) so that there are little air pockets between the fibers. This creates an insulating effect, determined by the yarns you use.

Originally, hand-knit sweaters were tube-shaped. The authentic Irish sweaters, for instance, had no seams. In Peru, sweaters are still knitted without seams by working with five needles and using circular knitting techniques.

Today sweaters usually consist of four separate pieces: front, back and two sleeves, which are assembled in

Fig. 23 A traditional close-fitting fisherman sweater, used mainly to protect against the cold.

Fig. 24 Knitwear is stretchable and can be assembled without seams or closures.

15

the end.
There are other possibilities though, which will be discussed later.

Stitches

In Fig. 27/28 you will see a close-up view of a swatch. By inserting a blunt yarn needle, the stitches of the swatch are duplicated. This technique is called duplicate stitch or Swiss darning and is used primarily for embroidering motifs. These samples are designed to make knitting principles clearer to you and to show that different stitches affect the size of the garment. For instance, in ribbing, the relationship between yarn and needles is different than in stockinette stitch. Also, the size of the garment is determined by the way your fingers control the yarn and the resulting tension or gauge. Thicker yarns require a slacker control of tension while thinner yarns require a tighter control. This is the reason a gauge swatch is always recommended (Fig. 29). Printed patterns usually give a gauge, stating the number of stitches and rows in a 4-inch square using the recommended yarn and needles. This information is also provided on the yarn label. By changing the recommended needle sizes, it is usually possible to obtain the suggested gauge if your swatch is bigger or smaller than a 4-inch square.

16

purl

Fig. 26 Wrong side of work in stockinette stitch, also known as reverse stockinette stitch when used as right side of work.

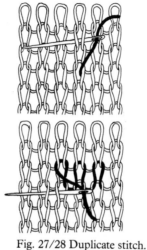

Fig. 27/28 Duplicate stitch.

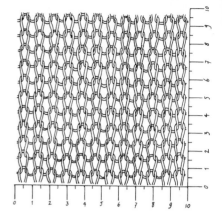

Fig. 29 Gauge swatch. It is necessary to knit a swatch of at least 4″ in your yarn and chosen stitches. Pin the swatch to a flat surface and count the number of stitches and rows in the 4″ section to see if the gauge is correct. A more detailed description of this is given on page 71.

knit

Fig. 25 Right side of work in stockinette stitch.

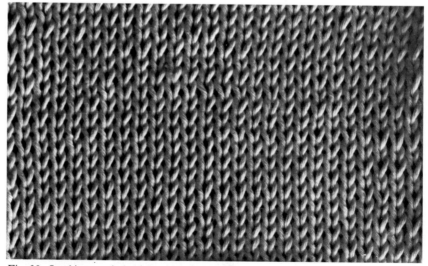

Fig. 30a Stockinette stitch (right side of work): Row 1: K. Row 2: P. Always repeat these two rows.

Fig. 30b Stockinette stitch (wrong side of work in Fig. 30a)

Fig. 30c Ribbing (even number of stitches): Row 1: K1, P1. Row 2: K all K sts, P all P sts. Always repeat these two rows.

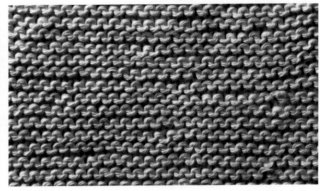

Fig. 30d Ribbing (multiple of 2): Row 1: K2, P2. Row 2: work the sts as they appear; that is K the K sts, and P the P sts. Repeat these two rows.

Fig. 30e Garter stitch: K all rows.

Fig. 30f Seed stitch (odd number of stitches): Row 1: *K1, P1*, rep, * to *, end with K1. Row 2: P the K sts, K the P sts. Always repeat these 2 rows.

Fig. 31 Condo knitting or River stitch: Row 1: K in size 9 needles. Row 2: K in size 1 needles. Always repeat these two rows.

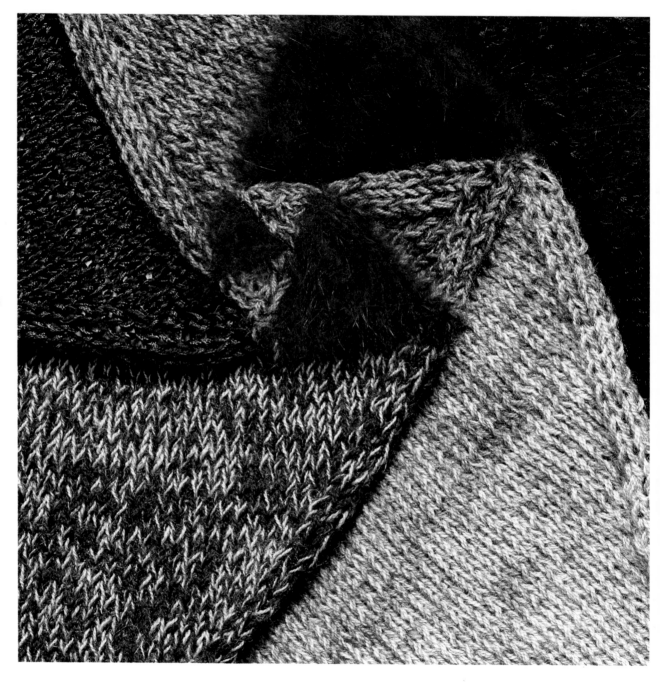

18

Materials

Even if you decide to work your design in one color, it is still possible to create an interesting pattern by using different yarns. In addition to wool and synthetic yarns, you can knit with cotton, string, ribbon, raffia or any pliable fiber. The knitted "wall" on page 13 would have looked completely different if knitted with yarn of a high luster. The specific textures of a yarn (soft, firm, hairy, smooth, supple, thick, thin, etc.) can have an enormous effect on the way the design is interpreted. The warm, soft and fluffy appearance of mohair and angora is a good example.

On the other hand, you could also take different kinds of yarn and place them next to each other for a contrasting effect. Look at the design in Fig. 32, where triangles form the basis of this sweater. Although many different yarns were used (wool, mohair, lurex, angora), there were only two colors (gray and blue).

If you look at the triangle design sweater on page 63, it is evident that color played the leading part in that design, not the materials.

Fig. 32 The contrasting effect in this sweater is achieved by using different types of yarn for each triangle. Decrease for the triangles as follows: K2, sl 1 Kwise, work to last 4 sts, K2 tog, K2. Decrease on right side of work only.

Fig. 33 Sweater in plaited basket pattern. Work as follows on an even number of stitches: Row 1: Pass in back of the first stitch on the left-hand needle and K the 2nd st through the back loop, then K the first 1st through the back loop, letting both sts drop off the LH needle together.
Row 2: P1, *pass in front of the 2nd st and P the next st, P skipped st, letting both sts drop off the LH needle together, work * to * across row, end with P1.
In this sweater the same stitch is used, but every 4 rows the bulky wool yarn is alternated with a thinner cotton yarn achieving a different effect with the same stitch.

Yarns

We mentioned earlier that knitted garments are stretchable. Depending on the construction of each yarn, the characteristics of knitwear may vary. Let us elaborate a little more on the construction of yarns.

Yarns are fibers spun into single threads. Although single threads are not very strong, they can be used for knitting. This should be done carefully and loosely, to prevent the threads from breaking. The final garment will be strong though, and the interrelation of the fibers in the stitches will give it a very special appearance. When two strands of yarn are spun together, it is called plying. Plying is usually done on a spinning wheel in two different ways.

One is twisting two strands around each other with the wheel turning in the same direction as it was turning when two strands were spun; the other is twisting two or more strands around each other with the wheel turning in the opposite direction as it was turning when the two strands spun. On a spinning wheel you have the ability to twist thin commercial yarns into yarns of your own color choice. Even without a spinning wheel you can combine yarns while knitting, by twisting the yarns around each other. The effects of twining, or twisting, can result in fancy and complex yarns. For instance, by adding twist to one of the single strands while reducing it in the other, little loops will be formed in the yarn; this type of yarn is called boucle. Or you could use strands of different colors or strands of a different thickness.

The yarns twisted on a spinning wheel will have a smoother texture than those twisted by hand, but the advantage of doing it by hand is that it is easier for you to control the design (color). Although novelty yarns are available in stores, combining your own yarns will give you unlimited possibilities. You could incorporate beads or feathers, or even knit with sewing thread or rags.

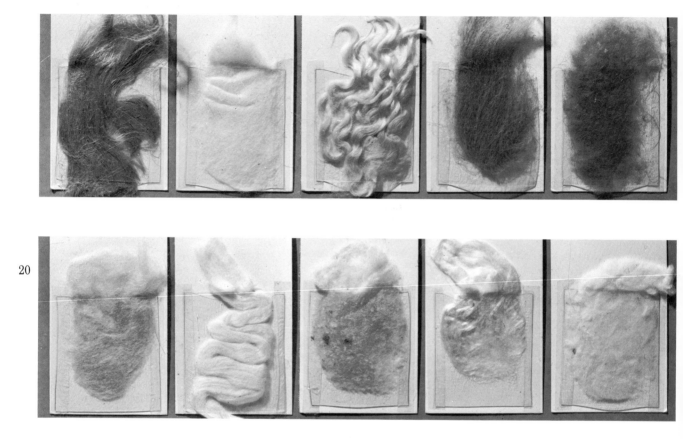

Fig. 34 Several natural fibers, from top left to right: jute, vegetable fiber; angora, animal fiber of the angora rabbit; mohair, animal fiber of the angora goat; alpaca, animal fiber of the alpaca; camel hair, animal fibers. From bottom left to right:, silk, animal fiber, unbleached; cotton batting, vegetable fiber; silk, animal fiber (rough silk); silk, animal fiber, bleached; cotton fluff, vegetable fiber.

Raw materials

When selecting yarn for a sweater, it is advisable to keep in mind what function the garment will serve. If it is made to protect against the cold, wool or a wool/synthetic combination will be the best choice. If the sweater will be worn and washed frequently, a synthetic yarn will be best. In evening wear, you could use novelty yarns such as lurex or angora.

Raw materials can be categorized as follows:

1. Natural fibers:
a. Animal (wool, silk, mohair, etc.)
2. Manmade fibers:
a. Vegetable (viscose, rubber, etc.)
b. Mineral (glass, aluminum, etc.)
c. Synthetic (acrylic, acetate, polyester, etc.).

Although viscose and rubber are extracted from vegetable fibers, the yarns are still manmade
Following is a description of the different yarns, their characteristics, and how to recognize them.

Animal fibers

Animal fibers include wool, silk and mohair. Protein is the raw material of all animal fibers. Testing animal fibers by burning smells like burnt hair and produces an irregular crisp black inflated mass. If, however, the remaining ashes smell like burnt hair, but leave a tar-like residue, it means that the yarn is a combination of wool and synthetic thread. These combinations, called "blends," are created to produce a strong yarn.

To distinguish silk from wool and hair, we have to look at the original fiber. Silk fibers are long, have a soft texture and are smooth. Wool and hair, on the other hand, are dull and kinky.
Wool is the product of sheep shearings. We're using "hair" to refer to the coats of all other animals. Wool is elastic and easy to work with and does not easily crease. It is not as strong as cotton or synthetic yarns, but is very durable because of its elasticity.
Wool sweaters should be handwashed in cold or lukewarm water and gently squeezed. Using hot water and/or agitation will result in shrinkage as the wool fibers kink more tightly. This is called matting or felting. Sometimes matting or felting is done deliberately to make the garment more dense and firm. The fishermen's sweaters mentioned earlier were usually knitted oversized (sometimes twice as large) and then shrunk by using hot water and agitation. Other types of hair are mohair from the Angora goat; cashmere from the undercoat of the Kashmir goat; alpaca, fine long woolly hair from the alpaca domesticated in Peru; and angora from the Angora rabbit. Their characteristics are more or less the same and most of them are relatively expensive.
Silk is a fiber obtained from the cocoon of the silkworm. It consists of two threads, each over 700 feet long. Compared to wool and hair, silk has an "endless" (continuous) fiber, known as filament. Silk fibers are thin and have a high tensile strength. Wrinkles will disappear quickly when the garment is hung on a hanger.
The silk fiber is smooth and is almost as effective an insulation as wool. Just like wool though, silk should be carefully handwashed. Keep in mind that knitted silk can stretch after washing.

Manmade fibers

Vegetable fibers are cotton, linen and rayon. Cellulose is the raw material of vegetable fibers. When burnt, these fibers smell like burnt paper and leave little or no ashes.
You can distinguish rayon from linen and cotton by soaking part of the rayon thread in water. When you pull the thread, it will break at the wet section. Linen or cotton, on the contrary, are stronger when wet and will break at the dry sections. When you look very closely at the fibers, it is easy to see the differences. The fibers of linen are coarse, with offshoots longer than two inches; cotton fibers are smoother and shorter. Rayon is a manmade fiber and can therefore have an endless thread. Sometimes these threads are cut short, but they still are smoother than those of cotton.
Cotton and linen fibers have almost the same characteristics. Cotton is stronger than wool, but weaker than linen. Cotton and linen do not stretch and are not crease-resistant. Cotton and linen are comfortably cool in summer. Both can be washed at high temperatures (white: up to 200^0F, colored: up to 140^0F). Rayon is weaker than cotton and not as good an insulator. It may be washed in hot water, but should be ironed at a lower temperature.

Synthetic fibers are laboratory-created and the result of petroleum byproducts. Most synthetic fibers will melt in the burning test and leave hardly any ashes. The threads (filament) are very long, but are often cut short to give them a better insulating capability.
Synthetic fibers are absorbent; as a result, they dry quickly; they are strong, elastic and crease-resistant. Because they are absorbent, they produce static and are easily soiled.

Colored synthetic fibers should be washed at 100^0F, whites at 140^0F.

4. TWO-DIMENSIONAL DESIGNING

In this chapter, knitted garments are visualized as a flat surface. This surface is shaped by using stitches, materials and colors. A well-balanced use of these elements is important. To achieve harmony in the design, you should know which visual elements are at hand and how to arrange them harmoniously in the design.

The arrangement of parts into an artistic form is called a composition. In making a composition on a flat surface we have to deal with the visual elements: color, structure, texture, line, surface and form. Each element will be discussed separately; then we will look at the different ways of putting elements together to attain unity throughout the design.

Color

When you choose colors for a knitting project, the selection you make depends on your "color sense." Besides being subject to tradition and current fashion trends, there are numerous aspects of color that may be unknown to us. Color is a very complex subject. What you should know is that there are three primary colors: red, yellow and blue. These form the basis for all other colors, such as the secondary and tertiary colors.
Orange is obtained by mixing red and yellow; green by mixing yellow and blue; purple by mixing red and blue. Those are the secondary colors. Tertiary colors are obtained

by further blending of two colors, one primary and one secondary. Pure color to which white is added is called a "tint" of that color. If black is added it is called a "shade." Mixing of colors is much easier in painting than in knitting. With yarns you are depending on the colors that are already dyed by the manufacturers. Of course, you could dye your own yarn with natural or synthetic dyes. To create color blends in knitted garments you

could use stitch variations or color overflows. We will give you some examples later.
Besides mixing colors you can also create color contrasts. When you take two colors, which are opposites on the color wheel, you obtain a strong contrast. If you want to obtain a softer contrast, you could select variations of one color, for instance, different hues of red. When you knit in different colors you have to deal with several balls of

Fig. 35 Striped motifs are technically easy. The pattern on the front is the same as on the back and the sleeves.

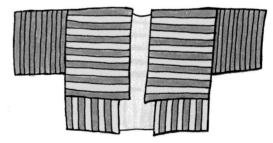

Fig. 36 In order to obtain horizontal as well as vertical stripes in the design, this sweater is composed of separate sections. Three colors are used: blue, yellow and red. Pay particular attention to the color blue: between the yellow stripes it has a greenish hue, while between the red stripes it almost looks purple.

Fig. 37 Johannes Itten's twelve-part color wheel. The primary colors are red, yellow and blue. When blended they become secondary colors: orange, green and purple.

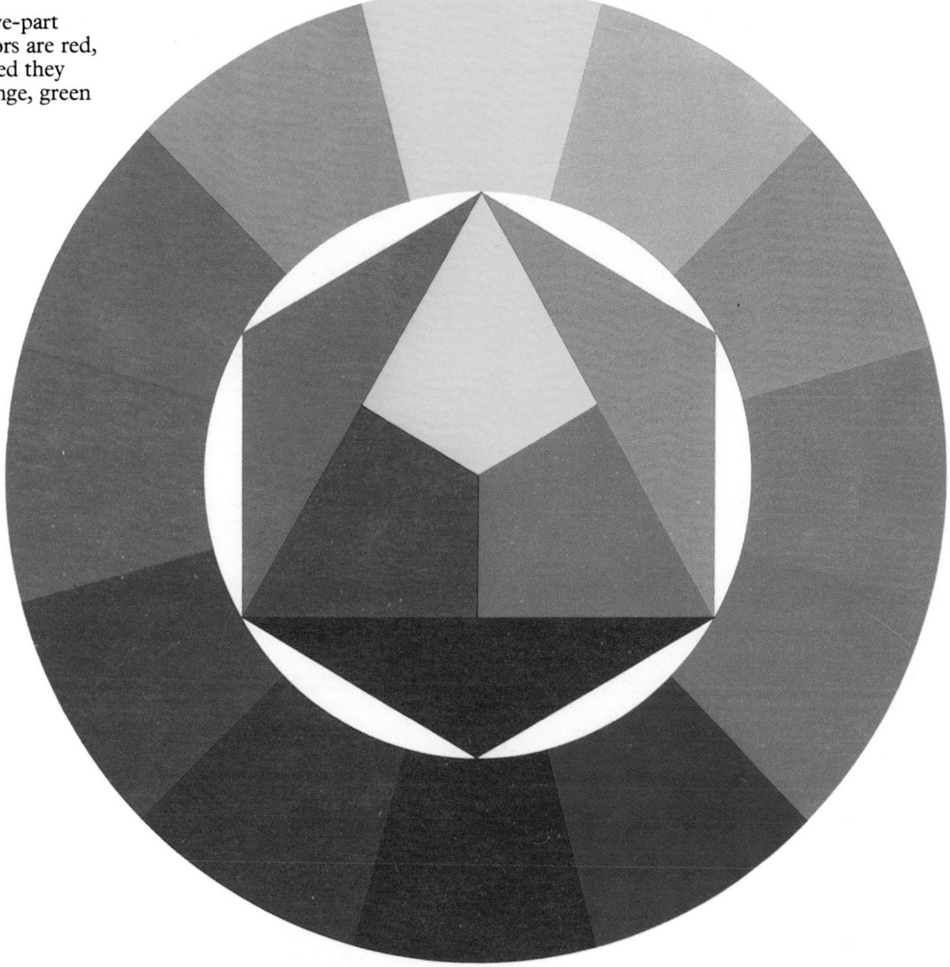

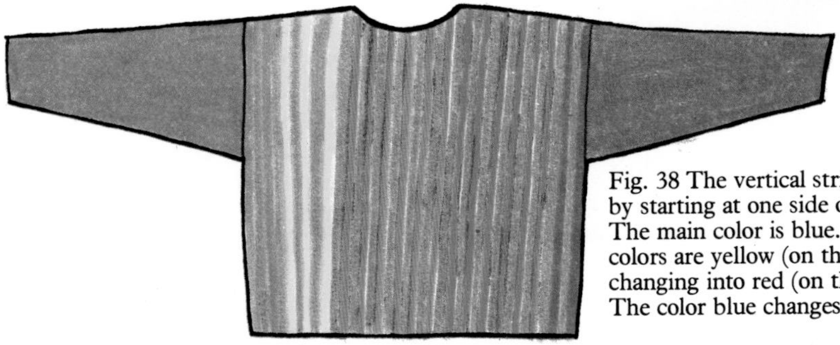

Fig. 38 The vertical stripes are obtained by starting at one side of the sweater. The main color is blue. The contrasting colors are yellow (on the left side), changing into red (on the right side). The color blue changes noticeably.

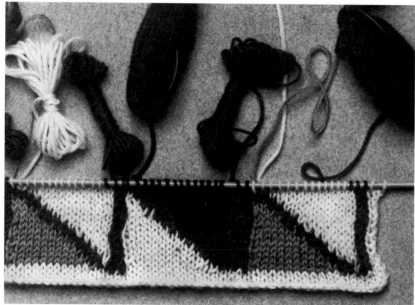

Fig. 39 Bobbins and butterflies are used to prevent tangling of the yarn in multicolored patterns.

the back of the sweater are prevented. When changing colors, the yarns are crossed around each other on the wrong side of the work.
2. If you work in small motifs, the strands can be carried loosely across the back of the work. Again, when changing colors, the strands will be crossed around each other and carried on the wrong side of the work. It is important to regulate the tension of the yarn as it is being carried across the back of the work, so that the motif is not distorted by pulling too tight. If the floats are too long they can catch on jewelry or buttons.

Floats greater than eight stitches long should be avoided; it is better to cross the yarns one time in the middle, i.e. after four stitches.
3. Multicolored motifs can also be worked in jacquard. This technique is discussed on page 28.

Color blends
Working with multicolored designs, you should know that the type of yarn you use is very important. For instance, if you mix two different colors of mohair, you will find out that this type of yarn mixes much better than cotton. It is worthwhile to take some time to find the right type of yarns in the right colors. Some people have lots of leftovers, gathered over the years, which can come in handy for selecting yarns and colors. Make sure the gauges of the different kinds of wool you choose are compatible with each other.

If you plan a design with sharp lines, for instance, mohair will not

yarn at the same time. Some people are afraid of this jumble of yarn, because it easily tangles. There are some tricks, though, to keep the strands separated, such as working out the design to avoid using too many balls at the same time. When working a horizontal striped pattern, for instance, you use one color at a time. The strands only need to be tied on at the beginning of the row. If the stripes are not very wide, you can just let the strands hang, but if they are wide, it may better to cut them off and darn all loose ends neatly into the selvage or through the back of the work. Especially when knitting small multicolored motifs, it is easier to

work with short strands, instead of carrying all the balls of yarn across. It may take more time at the end to weave in the ends, but knitting this way is much easier.

If you need strands of a considerable length, you may consider winding separate bobbins or butterflies of each yarn used (Fig. 39). To avoid weak spots and holes in the garment when working multicolored patterns, use one of the following three methods:
1. If you work large blocks of color in your design, take separate bobbins of yarn for each block. That way the strands do not have to be carried over from block to block and long strands or "floats" of yarn in

be suitable.

In Fig. 40 and 40a, examples are shown of very subtle color blends. The same type of yarn in five different shades of orange is used, three strands at a time. The procedure is as follows:

1. several rows with three strands of color 1;
2. several rows with two strands of color 1 and one of color 2;
3. several rows with one strand of color 1 and two strands of color 2;
4. several rows with three strands of color 2, etc.

When the designer realized that the colors 3 and 4 were still too far apart in color, the fourth color was incorporated every 4 stitches in one row, every 3 stitches the next row and every 2 stitches the next one until finally a complete row was worked in that color. Sometimes you can't find the right color. By combining yarns and knitting them together, a new color can be created. It is also possible to combine colors by using the same technique as the pointillists (stipplers) by painting (stippling) small color stripes (stitches) close to each other. You will see an example in Fig. 42. In the middle part of this swatch, the purl stitches are worked in pink and the knit stitches in orange.

Combining colors by using different stitches

By using stitches where the strands are not lying right next to each other, but cross each other, it is much easier to let contrasting colors run into one another. If you knit a sweater in stockinette stitch, the color flows are achieved by selecting subtle color shades. When different kinds of stitches are used, the colors will blend even more.

Extremely effective stitch variations are: weaving stitch, turk stitch, patent stitch, fisherman rib, tweed stitch (woven barred stitch), seed stitch and all other crossed stitches.

Color contrasts

When you experiment with color contrasts in your design, you will find that contrasts can have a relatively limited value. For instance, if you knit a large field in black, and incorporate only one white stripe, the contrast between those two colors is much greater than when you knit several alternating stripes of white on that same size black field. The size of the field plays an important role here. Contrasts can also be weakened by repetitious use of the same motif. Colors that are opposites on the color wheel (see Fig. 37) bring out the biggest contrast. These are called complementary colors, i.e. red-green, orange-blue, yellow-purple, etc. There used to be a clear-cut opinion about which colors would go together and which ones clash, but that is not so anymore. We got used to the shocking combinations of orange and pink, for example, that are popular with teenagers' clothing. We can even find some traces in more sophisticated clothing.

In fact, all colors that are not the same can work as contrasts, even colors that are shades of the same color, such as light and dark green.

Between the colors that are next to each other on the color wheel, there is a color harmony; for example: yellow-orange or orange-red.

If you add white, gray or black to a primary color, the primary color will change. You could soften a primary color by knitting a strand in a primary color together with ak white, black or gray one. A red square in a gray field looks different from one placed in a black field. Colors also have a psychological effect on people. You may want to consider this effect in your designs. Yellow and red are warm colors. They are called activating colors and are associated with life, youth or energy. They do not have the calming effect that blue has. Secondary colors do not have such strong characteristics. Green next to blue looks warm and next to yellow, cold.

Orange is warm because it is a mixture of yellow and red. There are many possibilities for multicolored patterns by using different crossed stitches. Strands of contrasting colors will partially overlap each other, so that the contrasting effect is lessened. If you want to make the contrast sharper, you can achieve that by using a contrasting stitch as well.

For example, small black squares in a white field will have more effect when they are knit in two different kinds of stitches. An even stronger contrast is obtained if you use a different type of yarn for each color.

Fig. 40 and 40a
Colors blends. The instructions are
given on page 25.

Fig. 41 Sweater with color blends. The
sweater consists of several separate
sections in different color blends, using
blue and gray lines as contrasting colors.
Two sections, each 38-1/2″ long and 7″
wide, go from the lower front over the
shoulders to the lower back. The two
middle sections, front and back, are 17-
1/2″ long and 9″ wide. The sleeves are
also composed of three sections. The
middle sections are 12″ long and 5-1/2″
wide. The two side sections are 8″ wide
at the armholes and 3″ wide at the
wrists.
To finish the sweater a small hem was
sewn at the bottom of the sleeves, the
neckline and the lower front and back
edges of the sweater.

Fig. 42 The color blend from pink to
orange is very subtle by alternting knit
and purl stitches. The knit stitches are
worked in orange, the purl stitches in
pink.

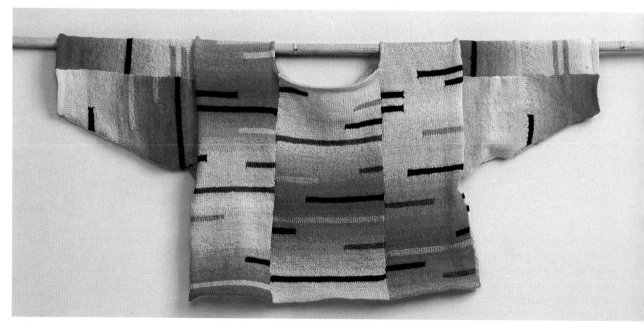

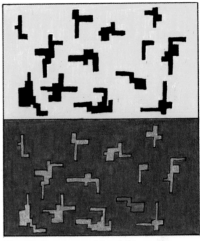

Fig. 45 Contrasts with small motifs. While the black and yellow form a strong contrast, the two shades of blue do not.

shows an even greater color blending than the first part.
4. The fourth part is worked in the woven barred stitch. The light and deep yellow rows are used for the background, while the violet strands are carried over the front, once every three rows.
5. The fifth part, worked in an openwork stitch, shows a zigzag pattern instead of horizontal lines. This effect is reached by increasing and decreasing stitches. In this sample it was worked as follows (multiple of 6 stitches):
Row 1: *yo, K2, K2 tog, K2*.
Row 2: Purl.
Row 3: *K2, K2 tog, K2, yo*.
Row 4: Purl.

Fig. 44 Contrasts in color can be sharp or very subtle. This swatch in stockinette stitch has a pattern repeat of five stitches in a different color. The background and the design are worked in the same three colors (light and deep yellow and blue). When light and deep yellow are used together, there is very little contrast. Combining blue with one of the two yellows results in a bold contrast.

Fig. 43 This picture clearly shows the effect of different stitches, when using the same color pattern of one row in violet, one row in deep yellow and one row in light yellow. The color sequence has been applied consistently throughout this swatch.
1. The first part is knit in garter stitch. Although each row is worked in a different color, double stripes of the same color appear. That's because in the garter stitch the loops from one row intertwine with the loops of the next one.
2. This is not the case in the second part, which is worked in stockinette stitch. The systematic color sequence is much clearer here.
3. The third part, worked in seed stitch,

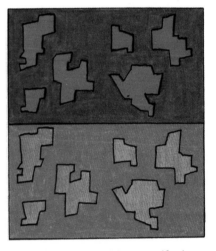

Fig. 46 By using even bigger motifs, the contrasting effect also becomes bigger.

Jacquard

The word "jacquard" is taken from the inventor of the same name, who invented a loom for weaving patterned fabrics. The system worked like a punch card reader. Jacquard can also be done on knitting machines that work with the same kind of punch card system. However, when hand knitting these motifs, a special technique, the weaving method, is used, in order to prevent long floats on the back of the sweater.

To work this method, put the right hand needle under the yarn color to be carried, before you work the next stitch. Knit only the working color through the stitch, catching the carried yarn at the back.

On the reverse side of the sweater (purl side), keep the yarn being used in front and pass the right hand needle one time under and one time over the carried yarn before purling the stitch.

This technique is often used in round or circular knitting, as all the rounds are worked on the knit side. Instead of using the weaving method, you can work jacquards in the crossed yarn method as explained on page 24.

Another method is embroidering or Swiss darning the motifs. The designs are worked in duplicate stitch on a finished stockinette background. The effect of the design worked this way may not be as clear as when you work it in the knitted jacquard technique, as the background will show. This can also be done intentionally by embroidering the design with a

28

Fig. 47 A painting from Picasso was used as the basis for a design. The straight lines and the square shapes are extremely suitable for a knitting design.

thinner yarn than the one you used for the background.

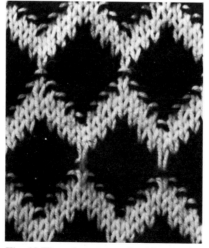

Fig. 48 The color contrast in this swatch becomes even more effective by also working the different stitches in a different color.

Fig. 49 Picasso sweater. With a square frame (see page 9), a particular fragment of the painting in Fig. 47 was selected. This part was transferred onto graph paper. A swatch should be knitted in order to determine the gauge of the yarn and the size of the needles. Put the counted rows and stitches on the graph paper and work out your color scheme. The sweater in this picture is made in one piece.

To make the increases for the sleeves, the sweater has been divided into two equal parts, so that the sleeves could be worked separately. This prevented having too many stitches on the needle. When the sleeves were finished, the back was knitted in one piece again (see also Fig. 2).

Fig. 52 Two different yarns (gray, thin, shiny cotton and gray angora), are knitted together in small squares of four stitches wide and four rows high. The result is a subtle contrast.

Fig. 53 In this swatch, a mint green yarn is used of two different weights, one a bulky woollen yarn (meant to be worked on size 8 needles), the other a thin woollen yarn (for size 0 needles). By knitting both yarns with size 3 needles in a block pattern, you can see that the blocks in the bulky yarn are raised from the surface, while the thinner yarn is drawn to the back. A relief stitch is the result.

Color and yarn

Some yarns absorb light and others reflect light. If you knit a sweater in one color, but use different types of yarn, you get a very interesting effect. You could, for instance, knit a sweater in stockinette stitch in a smooth yarn, and incorporate squares worked in mohair. Another possibility is to knit triangles in a glossy cotton on a background of a regular matte cotton. You could also change an existing pattern, designed for different colors, by using different kinds of yarn.

Structure and texture

For a better understanding of these two concepts, let's give a definition of both.

Structure: composition of small parts to form a whole. We mean the way in which a design or garment is arranged.

Texture: the visible and touchable surface of the knitted garment. the texture can change by varying the stitches and yarn. On the next pages we will explore the textural and structural changes achieved by using different stitches.

Fig. 50 Detail of jacquard sweater. Complementary colors are used that do not produce a strong contrast. The irregular motifs were drawn on graph paper and knitted accordingly.

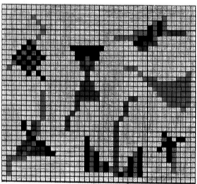

Fig. 51 Some motifs drawn on graph paper. As the motifs are far apart from each other, they are not knitted in, but embroidered later on the finished sweater.

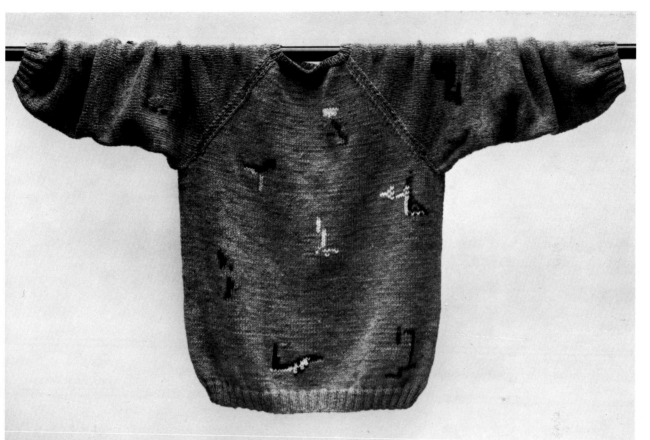

Fig. 54 Sweater with embroidered motifs, inspired by Miro.
Instructions.
Back: With size 4 needles, cast on 112 sts and work 1-1/2″ in K2, P2 ribbing. With size 7 needles, work in St st until work measures 17″. Shape raglans by binding off the following sts: At each edge of every 2nd row: bind off 6 sts 1 time, bind off 3 sts 1 time, bind off 2 sts 1 time. Then decrease 1 st at each edge of every 2nd row 26 times. The decreases at both edges should be made 4 sts from the edge of a row as follows: On the right, K4, sl 1 st as if to knit, K

the next stitch, pass the sl st over the K st, work to the last 6 sts, K2 tog, K4. Bind off remaining 38 sts.
Front: work same as back. When there are 46 sts left on the needle, shape neck as follows: bind off the 18 center sts and divide work into two equal parts. At each neck edge of every 2nd row, bind off 4 sts 1 time, bind off 3 sts 1 time, bind off 2 sts 1 time and decrease 1 st 1 time.
Sleeves: Cast on 62 sts with size 4 needles and work 1-1/2″ in K2, P2 ribbing. With size 7 needles work in St st, increasing 8 sts evenly spaced across

first row. Then increase 1 st at each edge every 1-1/2″ until there are 88 sts on the needle.
When work measures 20-1/2″, shape raglans by binding off at each edge of every 2nd row: 5 sts 1 time, 3 sts 1 time, 2 sts 1 time and 1 st, 26 times. Bind off the remaining 16 sts.
Neck border: with size 4 needles pick up sts and work 2-1/2″ in K2, P2 ribbing. Fold the neck band in half and sew it to neck.

Knit and purl stitches

A well-arranged structure can be obtained by working a pattern in knit and purl stitches. When alternating knit and purl stitches next to or on top of each other (for instance by using the seed stitch on page 17), it will affect the length or width of the sweater only slightly. However, if you use two or more of the same stitches next to or on top of each other, the length and width can be affected.

In ribbing, for instance (K1, P1, or K2, P2), the width will be smaller. The purl stitches are drawn to the back, so that they can hardly be seen; and the knit stitches are raised, so that vertical lines are formed on the right side of the sweater.

If you work horizontal lines (for example, K 2 rows, P 2 rows, K 2 rows, P 2 rows, etc.), the purl stitches will surface and the knit stitches are drawn back and become invisible on the right side of the sweater. The sweater will consequently be shorter. The specific characteristics of these stitch sequences can be used to obtain very interesting textures.

32

Fig. 55 Variations in knit and purl stitches:
Fig. a through d are knitted in one color only.

55 a. Blocks: Cast on 24 sts.
Rows 1 through 4: K4, P4
Rows 5 through 8: P4, K4

55 c. Cast on 24 sts.
Row 1 and 2: K2, P2
Row 3: K3, P4, K4, P4, K4, P4, K1
Row 4: P1, K4, P4, K4, P4, K4, P3
Repeat rows 1 through 4.
Note the relief effect of this pattern.

55 e. A diagonal motif in knit and purl stitches, worked in two colors.

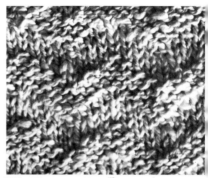

55 b. Zigzag motif in knit and purl stitches.

55 d. This swatch shows that purl stitches, horizontally used, come to the surface, while purl stitches vertically used are drawn to the back.

55 f. Alternating diagonal motif in two colors. Note that where the knit and purl stitches are on top of each other, the purl stitches in both colors stand out.

55 g. Stockinette stitch with stripes in garter stitch of variable lengths. The stripes are worked in dark blue on a light blue background. To prevent the light blue background from showing through, the dark blue stripes are each worked over two rows: knitwise in the first row, and purlwise in the next one.

55 h. Front: K3, P1,
Back: P3, K1.
Crossed motifs are incorporated in a different color.

Stitch variations

Actually, there are a limited number of stitches, but their variations are innumerable. Some basic principles will be discussed here and indications will be given of how you can vary these.

A lot of traditional stitches were developed by experimenting and were passed on from one generation to the next. Many of these are still used in current fashion. It can be a real challenge, though, to come up with your own variations. We will advise you how to go about that. In the following example we will show you how, by winding the yarn several times around the needle, you will get the "elongated stitch" or "lazy woman stitch," so called because knitting this way is extremely fast.

Elongated stitch (see Fig. 56a, 56b, 56c)

Working method: knit one stitch by inserting the right-hand needle into the front of the stitch loop and wrapping the yarn several times around the needle instead of once. Several loops will remain on the needle. On the wrong side of the sweater, only the first loop will be worked, letting the extra loops drop. In general, variations with stitches can be achieved by:
1. the stitch itself
2. the number of times the stitch is worked
3. the extent to which the stitch is combined with other stitches
4. the color of the yarn
5. the yarn itself
6. the size of the needle
Applying these six variations to the elongated stitch could lead to the following:
1a. wrap the yarn several times around the needle
b. work in a twisted knit stitch (inserting the needle through the back loop)
2. vary the wrapping of the yarn around the needle, so little "waves" will develop
3a. stockinette stitch
b. ribbing
c. openwork patterns (yarn-over stitches)
4a. stockinette stitch in a different color than the yarn you use to wrap around the needle
b. the "waves" worked in another color
5a. see 4a
b. see 4b
6. Create a different effect by working an occasional row in the elongated stitch in a larger size needle.
Thus it can be very interesting to experiment with a stitch in different ways.
Be sure to save the swatches you make and write a short description of how they developed.

Yarn-over stitches

Another basic stitch develops by placing the yarn, knit or purlwise, over the right-hand needle. Extra loops will be formed. By knitting these loops in the next row, an openwork pattern is produced. This is the yarn-over technique. It is important to remember that you actually are making stitch increases. In order to keep the width the same, these increases should be compensated for by decreases in the

33

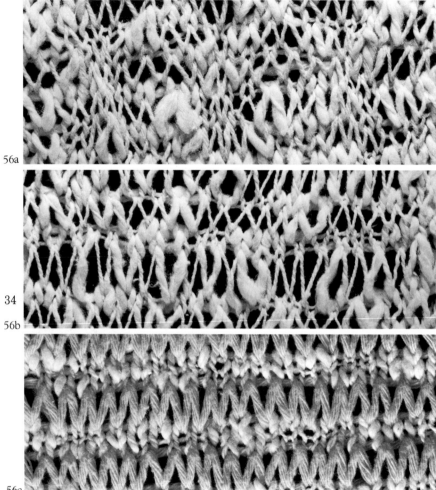

Fig. 56 Elongated stitch.
a. Row 1: sl 1 Kwise, K1, K1 (wrapping yarn 2 times around needle), K1 (wrapping yarn 3 times around needle), K1 (wrapping yarn 2 times around needle), K1, sl 1.
Row 2: Purl.
Row 3: K1 (wrapping yarn 3 times), K1 (wrapping yarn 2 times), sl 1 Kwise, K1 (wrapping yarn 2 times), K1 (wrapping yarn 3 times).
Row 4: Purl.

b. Row 1: Knit.
Row 2: Knit (wrapping yarn 2 times around needle for every stitch).
Row 3: Knit.
Row 4: Knit (wrapping yarn 3 times around needle for every stitch).
c. Rows 1 and 2: Knit in stockinette stitch in regular light pink cotton.
Row 3: Knit (wrapping yarn 2 times around needle for every stitch) in a bulky dark pink cotton.

same row or a later row.
Decreases can be made in two ways: knit stitches together or pass stitches over each other.
If two or more stitches are knit together, the loops worked in stockinette stitch on the front of the knitwear will slant to the right. By passing stitches over each other (slip 1 st as if to knit, K the next st, pass the sl st over the K st to the left) they will slant to the left.
Conclusion:
a. openwork patterns are made by creating extra loops in the yarn over technique.
b. slanted lines are formed in the garment when you make decreases as described above.
If you make a double decrease (sl 1 st, K 2 tog and pass the sl st over the st made by the K2 tog), 2 stitches are decreased. In order to compensate you should increase two stitches. This can be done as follows: Yarn over, one double decrease as just described, yarn over. These yarn over loops can also be made somewhere else in the row. For instance: yarn over, K 2, 1 double decrease, K 3, yarn over.
Innumerable variations are possible. The yarn over technique is an old one in the history of knitting and is used in very complicated openwork patterns. Real pieces of art were created that have a striking resemblance to lace (Fig. 59).
As a matter of fact, we encourage knitters to try duplicating an old lace pattern. It would be a shame if this craft were to disappear.
To come up with your own variations, we advise you to work according to the plan given on page 33.

57a   57b   57c

Fig. 57 Openwork pattens (yarn-over stitches)

a. Double decrease: yo, K1, double decrease (equals sl 1 st K2 tog, pass the sl st over the st made by the K2 tog), K1, yo.

b. Double decrease with yarn-over loops at a different place: yo, K3, double decrease, K3, yo, k1.

c. Multiple of 11 stitches.
Row 1: Purl (right side of work).
Row 2: Knit.
Rows 3, 5 and 7: *K2 tog, K3, yo, K1, yo, K3, K2 tog*.
Rows 4, 6 and 8: Purl.
Repeat these 8 rows for pattern.

d. Multiple of 6 stitches.
Row 1: *sl 1 Kwise, K3, yo, K2 tog, K1, K2
Row 2: K1, K3, yo, K1 (tog with loop of row 1), K1, K2*
Repeat these 2 rows for pattern.

35

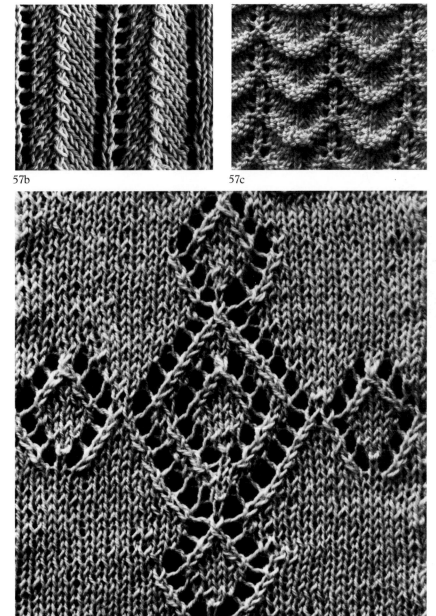

Fig. 58 An openwork pattern with a symbolic meaning: the eye of God. It was sometimes incorporated in fishermen's sweaters to ensure God's protection for fishermen.

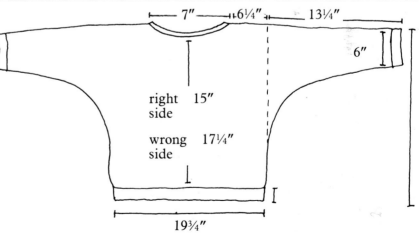

Fig. 60 Sweater with diagonal lines and openwork pattern.
The sweater is made in one piece. The stitches consist of an eyelet pattern resulting in diagonal lines.
Right side of work: ★K7, P2, K1, yo, sl 1, K1, psso, K2 tog, yo, K1, P2★.
Wrong side of work: K1, ★K2, P6, K2, P7★.
To continue in pattern, move 1 stitch to the right on every odd-numbered row.

7" ― 6¼" ― 13¼"

6"

right side   15"

wrong side   17¼"

19¾"

Fig. 61 Measurements of the sweater of Fig. 60. Make a gauge swatch in the yarn chosen and calculate the stitches and rows to determine the gauge of the yarn and the needles to be used.

Fig. 59 Antique knitted lace, a real work of art.

Fisherman Rib stitches

The fisherman stitch is used mostly for sweaters in one color. Garments made in this stitch have a raised surface and are very elastic. Because of this characteristic, sweaters knit in this stitch can sag, especially if they are worn a lot. You could knit the fisherman stitch in two colors; then the right side will have a different color from the wrong side.

If the seams are neatly finished, a sweater in this stitch can be worn on both sides. The working method of a two-color fisherman stitch is given in Fig. 62. Other fisherman stitches are:

Half-brioche or Tunisian Rib (uneven number of stitches):

Row 1: selv st, P1, *K1, P1*, repeat * to *, selv st.

Row 2: selv st, K1, *sl 1 Pwise, yo, K1*, repeat * to *, selv st.

Row 3: selv st, P1 *K2 tog (the yo and sl st of previous row), P1*, repeat * to *, selv st.

Repeat rows 2 and 3.

Mock fisherman stitch or English Rib (multiple of 4 stitches):

Row 1: *K3, P1*, repeat

Row 2: *K2, P1, K1*, repeat

Repeat these two rows.

Brioche or patent stitch (uneven number of stitches):

Row 1: *P1, K1*

Row 2: *K1, sl 1 Pwise, yo*, rep * to *, K1

Row 3: *yo, sl 1 Pwise, K2 tog (the yo and sl st of previus row)*

Repeat row 3 for pattern.

The same effect can be achieved by using the following stitch (beaded

38

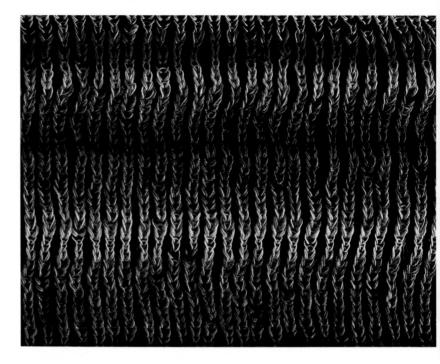

Fig. 62 Fisherman stitch in two colors.

Use double-pointed needles. In principle the stitch is similar to K1, P1 ribbing. On the reverse side, the stitches are worked as they appear on the needle.

Cast on in black and K 1 row.

1. In black: *K1, 1 double prl (by putting the RH needle into the center of the st below the next st to be worked and let both sts drop off the needle together)*. Do not turn work, but slip the sts back to the beginning of the needle (this is the reason for using double-pointed needles). With the contrasting color, work as follows: *1 double knit (K1 in the st below the st to be worked and let both sts drop off the needle), P1*. Turn work.

2. In black: *1 double knit (K1 in the st below), P1*.

Do not turn work, but slip the sts back to the beginning of the needle again.

In the contrasting color: *K1, 1 double purl (P1 in the st below)*.

Repeat 1 and 2 for pattern.

The contrasting colors in this sample are: beige, brown and gray.

Fig. 63 Sweater in different fisherman stitches

Gauge: Using size 6 needles: 4″ = 22 stitches x 30 rows.

The sweater consists of diagonal blocks in two different stitch patterns. The vertical and diagonal stripes are worked in stockinette stitch (K 1 row, P 1 row). To continue the pattern for the diagonal lines, shift 1 st to the left in every row. Because the stitches for the blocks are staggered, every row starts with a different stitch. The best way to find out is to knit a sample first.

Stitches used:

Bee cell stitch:
Row 1: *K1, 1 double stitch (= insert RH needle into center of the st below the next st to be worked and K1 letting both sts drop off the needle)*.

Row 2: *With the RH needle pick up the loop of the double st from the 1st row and K this one together with the following stitch, K1*.

Row 3: *1 double st, K1* (as in row 1, but note that this row starts with a double st instead of K1).

Row 4: As row 2 but start with K1.

Repeat these four rows for pattern.

Waffle stitch:
Row 1: K1, 1 double st (see bee cell stitch).
Row 2: Knit.
Row 3: 1 double st, K1.
Row 4: Knit.
Repeat these four rows for pattern.

Back and front:
With size 3 needles, cast on 110 sts and work 1-1/2″ in K2, P2 ribbing. With size 6 needles continue in block pattern. In this sweater the blocks are each 18 sts wide. The total length consists of seven blocks, with half a block at the bottom and half a block at the top. Use your own stitch variations in creating the blocks. After the block pattern, work 1-1/2″ in K2, P2 ribbing and bind off all stitches.

Sleeves:
With size 3 needles, cast on 48 sts and work 1-1/2″ in K2, P2 ribbing. Continue with size 6 needles in the bee cell stitch, increasing 8 sts evenly spaced across the first row. Beginning with the 8th row, increase 1 at each edge. Repeat these increases every alternate 10th and 8th row, until a total of 18 sts has been increased. When work measures 18″ bind off sts.

rib) with an even number of stitches:

Row 1: K

Row 2: *K1, 1 double st (insert the RH needle into the center of the st below the next st to be worked; knit a stitch through this st and let both sts drop off the needle together) Repeat row 2 for pattern.

Crossed stitches

Usually stitches are worked in the order they appear on the needle. It is possible, though to skip one or more stitches and knit others first. In order to do so, you could use a double-pointed or cable needle on which you slip several stitches, holding them on the front or the back of the work. This depends on how you want the stitches to be crossed. If the stitches on the extra needle are in back, the crossing will slant to the right; in front they form a crossing to the left.

Cable patterns belong to the category of crossed stitches. The cables are mostly worked in stockinette stitch on a purled background.

If you cross only one or two stitches you do not really need the extra needle.

Besides the traditional patterns with crossed stitches where they form rows of two or more stitches that run through each other, you could also create diagonal lines. See the sweater on page 42 for an example.

40

Fig. 64a Multiple of 14 + 6.
Row 1: *P6, sl next 4 sts to cable needle (cn) and hold in front, K4, K4 from cn*, repeat * to *, end with P6.
Rows 2 thru 6: Work stitches as established.
Row 7: *P6, sl next 4 sts to cn and hold in back of work, K4, K4 from cn*, repeat * to *, end with P6.
Rows 8 to 12: Work sts as established. Repeat from Row 1.

Fig. 64b Multiple of 14.
Row 1: *P2, sl next 2 sts to cn and hold in front, K2, K2 from cn, P2, K6*
Rows 2 and 4: Work stitches as established.
Row 3: Like Row 1.

Fig. 64c Multiple of 10 + 2.
Rows 1, 3, 5, 9 and 11: Knit.
Rows 2, 4, 6, 8, 10, 12, 14: Purl.
Row 7: selv st, *sl next 2 sts to cn and hold in front of work, K2, K2 from cn, K6*, K1.
Row 13: selv st, *K6, sl next 2 sts to cn and hold in back of work, K2, K2 from cn*, K1.
Repeat rows 3 to 14 for pattern.

Fig. 65 Variations of crossed stitches in 2 colors.

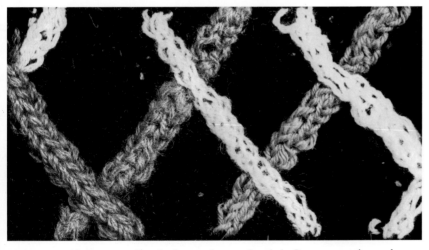

Fig. 66 On a black reverse St st background, green bands in St st are crossing each other.

These bands are made by using the same principle as used in cable patterns.

To cross the cable to the right, sl one P st at right edge of the cable, to a cn, and hold in back of work, K the green sts of the cable and then P the st from the cn.

To cross the cable to the left, sl the sts of the cable to a cn and hold in front of work, P1, and then K the sts from the cn.

Fig. 67 Baby sweater, size 12 months.
Materials: 250 grams cotton.
In this sweater diagonals of varying lengths are made. The diagonals are 11 sts apart. The length, distance and color of the diagonals can be varied, of course.
Gauge: using size 4 needles: 4″ = 25 sts x 30 rows in St st.
Front: with size 3 needles, cast on 60 sts and work in K1, P1 ribbing. Continue with size 4 needles and work in St st increasing 4 sts evenly spaced across the first row. In this sweater, the cable in the middle is started after 40 rows of St st.

The sweater is made in one piece. After 45 rows of St st, stitches are cast on for the sleeves at each edge as follows: 20 sts 1 time, 16 sts 1 time. You now have a total of 136 sts. After 67 rows the neck is shaped as follows: bind off the center 8 sts and divide work into two equal parts. At each neck edge of every 2nd row bind off 3 sts 2 times and 2 sts 1 time. On the left shoulder, 2 or 3 buttonholes are evenly spaced over a total of 20 sts at the neck edge. After making the buttonholes, bind off these 20 sts and cast them on again to work the back of the sweater. To shape the neck at the

back, cast on 3 sts 1 time, 4 sts 1 time at each neck edge of every 2nd row. Then cast on 10 sts at the center and rejoin both halves. When the sleeves, measured from the wrists, are 56 rows high, bind off 16 sts 1 time and 20 sts 1 time at each edge. Work the back the same as the front and bind off the stitches. To finish, with size 3 needles pick up sts from the neck and work 1″ in K1, P1 ribbing.

Fig. 68 Stitches and color.
An example of using different kinds of yarn: pink cotton and a mixed pink yarn of viscose, mohair, wool and polyamide. The swatch is worked in the linen stitch, which resembles the way fabric is woven. Procedure:
Row 1: with first yarn *K1, yarn in front, sl 1 Pwise, yarn in back*, rep.
Row 2: with 2nd yarn *P1, yarn in back, sl 1 Pwise, yarn in front 8, rep.
Although the yarns are similar in color, there is still a subtle contrast because of the different textures of the yarn.

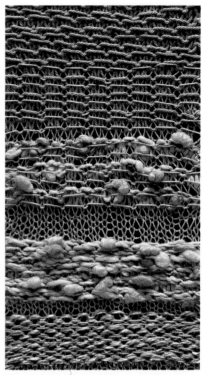

Fig. 69 Variations of the woven barred stitch using different materials in one color.

Looping

Another type of stitch is one where loops are formed on the front of the sweater. In order to make this stitch, the thread is carried over one or more stitches on the front. The stitches that are skipped are slipped off purlwise. This will give a woven or embroidered effect. An example is the woven barred stitch, used in the "wall" of the sweater on page 13.
On this page you can see other variations of this theme.

Woven barred stitch

This stitch is worked as follows:
Right side: *K1, yarn forward, sl 2 Pwise*

Reverse side: *P1, yarn back, sl 2 Kwise*

Stitches and color

When alternating knit and purl stitches, as in ribbing, the purl stitches are drawn to the back. This is also the case in the sweater on page 46. However, in this sweater, you will notice that at irregular intervals, some purl stitches are worked in loose double-stranded yarns in a different color; they are actually lying on top. The strands used are about a foot long. They hang loose on the back of the sweater until they are needed. When finished with the loose stradns, you should tie their ends (which are about an inch long on each side) in a knot at the loop of the adjoining stitch on the wrong side of the sweater. You can see that the colors

used in this sweater are arranged in a very harmonious way. The structure of the sweater is irregular. The colored purled stitches are at irregular intervals. The texture is also iregular. The purl stitches worked in the white yarn do not show, but the colored purl stitches do.

44

Fig. 70 Variation of the woven barred stitch in two colors.

Fig. 70a Variation of the woven barred stitch in three colors.

Fig. 70b Multiple of 3.
*Row 1: sl 1 Kwise, K2, yo, pass the sl st over the 3 sts.
Row 2: Purl*.
Repeat these two rows for pattern, alternating colors as desired.

Fig. 70c Multiple of 4.
*Row 1: K1, K2 tog, K1.
Row 2: K1, with RH needle pick up loop lying on first row and K, K1, K1.
Row 3: Knit.
Row 4: Purl*.
Repeat these four rows for pattern.

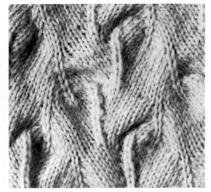

Fig. 71 Changing of direction.
Stitches can change direction when increases and decreases are made. If there are as many increases as decreases the number of stitches stays the same. In this swatch double decreases and double increases are alternated, with seven stockinette stitches in between. Double increase: K1, K1 into the stitch below. K1, K1 into the stitch below, K1. You now have 5 sts instead of 3. Double decrease: Slip 2 sts Kwise, K1 and pass the 2 sl sts over the K st.

Fig. 72 Structure/texture and material.
In this swatch you can see the effect of adding a different type of yarn when knitting the same bobble pattern stitch.
On the lower part, the pattern is worked in the same yarn and the effect is hardly noticeable, but in the second part a novelty yarn of cotton and viscose is added to knit the bobbles and the effect is accentuated. Procedure: In one stitch, work 4 sts: P1, K1, P1, K1. Pass the 4th st over the 3rd, pass the 3rd st over the 2nd and the 2nd over the first st. The bobble pattern is worked on a Stockinette st background.

Relief
In this book, relief knitting means knitting in which the surface is raised or lowered by using certain stitches. In some cases it is obtained by using a combination of knit and purl stitches (see Fig. 55). Furthermore, relief is very noticeable in cable patterns, bobble and embossed patterns and fisherman rib stitches.
If the garment calls for a relief surface, this can be done by increasing stitches and knitting a double layer on top of the existing one. Actually this is the principle used for knitting a pocket (see page 86). Another way to knit in relief is knitting double knits. Twice as many stitches are cast on as actually needed for the width. The stitches are worked in turns (every other one), so two layers will be obtained. A polyester batting can be put between the two layers, and the layers can then be knit together. This procedure is described on page 48.

Fig. 73 Relief knits are easy to make. In this swatch, worked in light and dark blue blocks, the threads in back are pulled extra tight on purpose, so that the blocks get a puckered effect.

Fig. 74 White sweater.
The sweater is worked in the following stitch pattern. On the right side of work: K3, P1. On the wrong side: P3, K1. A very special effect is obtained by using multicolored double stranded yarn on various purl stitches throughout the sweater instead of the white yarn. A lot of yarn will be hanging loose in the back of the sweater, which should be tied together, rather than bound off. To obtain an uninterrupted design, the sweater is made in one piece. A 100% cotton yarn is used with size 6 needles. For this size 8/10 sweater 56 sts were cast on. After 1-1/2″ in K1, P1 ribbing, the sweater was worked in the stitch pattern described above. At each edge of every right side of work row, 1 st is increased until the sweater measures 8″. Then increase 5 sts at each edge until there are 156 sts. When the sleeves are 13 rows high, at sleeve end, shape

shoulder. At the wrist edge bind off 5 sts at the beginning of every wrong side of work row, until there are no stitches left. Work the back the same as the front. The back and front are connected by a 4″-wide ribbing band. This will give the sweater more elasticity. Neck and sleeves are finished with K1, P1 ribbing.

Fig. 75 Triangles.
The stitches of the triangles in this swatch are picked up from the black background. They are then worked separately, creating an appliqued effect. The triangles are 17 sts wide at the base. The decreases are made the same way as on fig. 108 (page 62). When working on the triangles, the black sts should be placed on a double pointed needle. When the triangles are finished, except for 1 st, the black background is worked on and the remaining sts (one per triangle) of the triangles are slipped onto

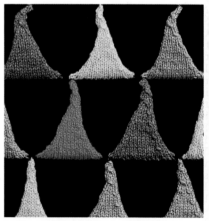

holders. The black background is worked until it is the same length as the triangles. The remaining sts of the triangles are then incorporated again.

Fig. 76 Baby sweater, size 12 months.
Materials: 250 grams cotton.
Stitches: Work the first 5 rows in St st.
On every 6th row, let every 4th st drop
from the needle and unravel for 5 rows,
then pick it up again across the front.
Long loops are formed. Work the next 5
rows in St st. On the 12th row the
intentionally dropped stitches should be
repeated, but they should be staggered
between the ones dropped in row 6.
Repeat these 12 rows for pattern.
Front and back:
With size 1 needles cast on 66 sts and
work 8 rows in ribbing. Continue with
size 3 needles in pattern st.
Back: When work measures 11-1/4",
bind off 18 sts at the left shoulder and
slip the 30 center sts onto a holder.
Work 6 more rows on the remaining 18
sts.
Front: When work measures 10-1/2",
slip the 16 center sts onto a holder and
shape the shoulders as follows.

Right shoulder: 25 sts remain. At the
neck edge of every other row, slip onto a
holder 3 sts 1 time and 2 sts 2 times.
Continue pattern for 6 or 7 more rows
and bind off remaining sts.
Left shoulder: Work same as right
shoulder. Work 3 buttonholes after work
is 1/2" high.
Sleeves: with size 1 needles, cast on 36
sts and work 8 rows in ribbing.
Continue with size 3 needles in pattern,
increasing 16 sts evenly spaced across
the first row. When work measures 8-
3/4" bind off sts.
Finishing: Sew pieces together.
Collar: Pick up all sts from holders.
With size 1 needles work in ribbing.
After 1/2" in ribbing, work one
buttonhole at the right side of collar.
after 1-1/4" bind off all sts.

Double knits
It seems complicated to knit several
layers at the same time, but if you
work a sample in colors first, you
will see that it is really not that
difficult.
To start, cast on twice as many
stitches as you need for the width.
Let us assume that the main color .
you use is blue and the other is
yellow. Start with the first row: K1
in blue, yellow yarn in back, K1 in
yellow, yellow yarn forward. The
second row: if the yellow yarn needs
to be worked, it should be brought
forward, P1, yellow yarn back, P1 in
blue. This procedure can be used
with many of the stitches described
in this book.
It is essential that the parts that are

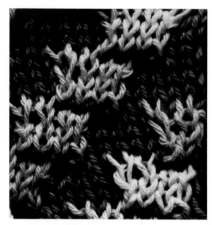

Fig. 77 Woven bars.
In order to obtain a woven effect as
shown, first work about 15 rows in St st.
With an extra set of needles, stitches are
picked up in the 5th row from the
bottom on the right side of work, in the
following order: pick up 5 sts, skip 3 sts,
pick up 5 sts, etc. These picked up
stitches are each worked for 10 rows,
until they measure the same as the
background. The picked up sts are then
incorporated with the stitches of the
background, in the same order as they
were picked up. The vertical bars are
now connected to the sweater.
Finally, the horizontal bars are made by
picking up stitches at the right edge of
the sweater. When they are the required
length, they are taken off the needle.
Then they are woven through the
vertical bars by hand and the stitches are
slipped back on the needle and sewn to
the side stitches. Bind off.
Stockinette stitch has a tendency to curl
up. This characteristic was used as an
extra feature for this design. If you look
at the bars, you will see that they almost
look as if they were knitted on a
spoolknitter.

Fig. 78 Double knit.
Double knits (4 stitches wide and 3 rows
high) are incorporated into this
turquoise sweater in St st. The little
rectangles look slanted wherever 4
stitches on the needle were pulled back
in order to knit the Stockinette st
background at the same time.

worked in double knit should be
twice as thick as the rest of the
knitwear, so that the surface is
raised. This effect can be increased
by filling these parts with a polyester
batting.
With double knits, it is possible to
have the front and back of the
knitwear look exactly the same; for
instance the right side of the
stockinette stitch can show on both
sides. In clothing where both sides
are visible, this type of knitting is
extremely suitable. A different effect
can be obtained if you choose a
contrasting color for the front.
When incorporating just a part in
double knit on a stockinette
background, the garment will
pucker slighty at the place where
this is incorporated, because part of
the stockinette stitches have to be

Fig. 79 Blocks in yellow and pink in
double knit

Fig. 79 Blocks in yellow and pink in
double knit
Cast on 30 stitches.
Row 1:
Block 1: P1 (in pink), put both yarns in
back, K1 (in yellow), put both yarns in
front (repeat 5 times).
Block 2: K1 (pink), yarns in front, P1
(yellow), yarns in back (repeat 5 times).
Block 3: K1 (yellow), yarns in front, P1
(pink), yarns in back (repeat 5 times).
Row 2:
Block 1: P1 (yellow), yarns in back, K1
(pink), yarns in front (repeat 5 times)
Block 2: K1 (yellow), yarns in front, P1
(pink), yarns in back (repeat 5 times).
Block 3: yarns in front, P1 (yellow),
yarns in back, K1 (pink) (repeat 5
times).
Repeat first and 2nd rows unti you reach
the desired length of the blocks. In this
example each block is 4 rows high. Then
the colors are alternated, so that yellow
blocks will come on top of pink blocks
and vice versa.

used to make the double knit. A
relief is formed.

48

Line, surface and form

On the preceding pages the elements of color and structure/texture were described. When designing an unpatterned sweater, the most important elements are color, stitches and yarn. As soon as you want to incorporate a design though, you have to deal with elements of line and plane.

If you look at Fig. 80 through 88, you will see these elements used in Islamic patterns. The motifs used are those applied in the art of Islam, such as architecture, weaving, knitting, embroidery and ceramics. They are not meant just for decoration, but are a reflection of arranging the cosmos by means of geometrical figures. These well thought out motifs can be a good starting point for yur own designing. Artists like Peter Struycken (see Fig. 88) are even making designs on computers. Other artists are investigating the possibility of visual patterns according to mathematical principles.

80a

80b

80c

80d

Line variations on an Islamic motif:
Fig. 80a The original drawing.

Fig. 80b Placing a piece of tracing paper on the drawing, you can trace some of the lines and use them for your design. This way the details of the motif disappeared, but the unity of lines was maintained.

Fig. 80c Other lines have been traced, but here they are heavier.

Fig. 80d The lines in this figure are so heavy that they form individual shapes.

Fig. 81 Shapes.
These shapes were also derived from
Fig. 80a. The primary colors yellow, red
and blue were used.

50

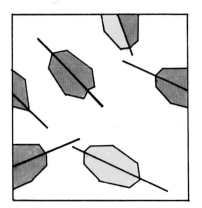

Fig. 82 Lines and shapes.
Shapes traced from Fig. 80a, divided by
lines.

Swatches in which another Islamic motif
was used:

Fig. 83a The motif is worked in coral
lines and shapes on a green background.

Fig. 83b The same design was used in
this swatch, but this time only one color
was used. The motif developed by using
knit and purl stitches.

Fig. 83c Lines and shapes from the same
motif.

83a

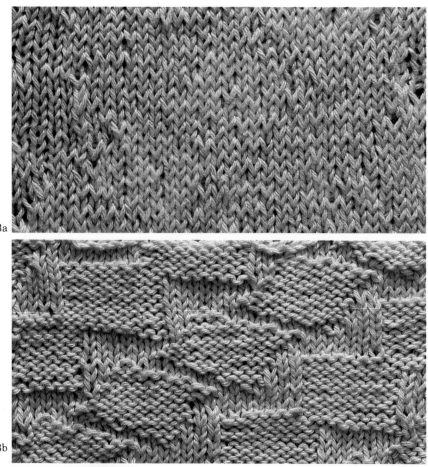

83b

83c

83d

Fig. 83d The fanciful motif of Fig. 83c
applied to a sweater.

Fig. 85 The door of the French house has been chosen to use as a motif for a design. By repeating the same motif, a block pattern developed that is easy to apply to a sweater.

Fig. 84 Instead of using an existing drawing of a motif, a photo can be used as a starting point. This is a photo of the facade of a French house, painted in neutral colors. The door has a colorful screen in front of it.

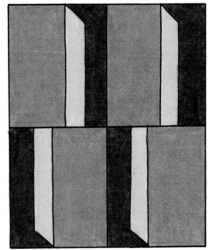

Fig. 87 The window to the right of the door has been repeated four times in a different color scheme, resulting in an abstract design.

Fig. 86 The screen of the door was used for another design. The squares are marked out on graph paper.

Composition

It seems complicated to arrange colors, lines, forms and stitches on a surface, but we can give you some rules that might be useful.

Repetition: Generally it is advisable to use a color, stitch or form more than one time in the design. The coherence of the design will be so much greater if, for instance, you embroider a certain triangle on the front of the garment and then repeat this triangle somewhere else, e.g., on the back or the sleeve. The shape of the triangle does not necessarily have to be the same; also the color may be different. It creates even a more interesting aspect if variations in color and shape are applied.

Direction: The shape of the design can also be placed in a different direction (see Fig. 91). We speak of incidental patterns when the same shapes are scattered on different parts of the sweater.
Technical note: when incorporating motifs randomly it is advised, especially when working in different colors, not to carry the threads over the back of the sweater. It is easier to work with bobbins or butterflies of the yarn. You could also embroider the motifs on the sweater in duplicate stitch after it is finished.

Rhythm: A rhythmic composition can be obtained when the same motifs are repeated in such a way that they interrelate with each other.

Size: By either enlarging or reducing the shapes, you could get another variation. For instance, when you plan to use a block pattern in your sweater, an interesting effect could be obtained by varying the size of the blocks.

52

Fig. 88 Peter Struycken's computer structure 4a, 1969.

Fig. 89 An Islamic motif on which the other designs on this page were based.

Fig. 90 Repetition: Derived from the motif in Fig. 89, this shape, in which a tiny square and a triangle were placed, was selected. Enlarged, these shapes can be applied several times on a sweater. The use of repetition often results in balanced composition.

Fig. 91 Direction: A small shape was repeatedly used in two colors. By placing the shapes in different positions, the composition gives the suggestion of movement.

53

Fig. 92 Rhythm: A shape from Fig. 89 was repeatedly used in groups of three. A rhythmic pattern is the result.

Fig. 93 A rhythmic pattern with triangles.

Fig. 94 Jacquard worked according to the graph paper design in Fig. 86.

Overlapping: A shape can become very intriguing when you let it partially overlap either the same shape or a different one. The two shapes together become a totally new shape (Fig. 95).

Enlarging: It is also possible to enlarge just a part of a picture. In this case you could make use of a square frame as we earlier discussed on page 7. In working out a design like this, the original picture is not recognizable anymore.

Fig. 95 Overlapping: Overlapping motifs instead of placing them next to each other is a simple way of obtaining a pleasing, balanced composition.

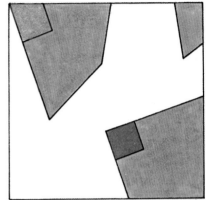

Fig. 96 Enlarging: A portion of Fig. 92 is enlarged. The rhythmic element of Fig. 92 almost disappeared in this enlargement, and a completely new composition was created.

55

Fig. 97 The motifs of the swatches in Fig. 83 were enlarged for this design and worked in knit and purl stitches.

Residual shaping: If you cut a triangle out of a piece of paper, you will have two shapes: the triangle and the residual piece of paper with the triangle missing. You could use both of these shapes in your design. In varying different shapes and their residuals you can make it even more interesting when you either enlarge or reduce the sizes of both of these and combine them in your design (Fig 98).

Symmetry: In a composition, when two figures form each other's mirror image, we speak of symmetry. In Fig. 99 you can see a symmetrically filled-in design. However, by using different colors, the composition becomes nevertheless asymetrical.

56

Fig. 98 Shapes and residual shapes: When a certain shape is used in a composition, there will always be a part left with "nothing." This is called the residual shape. It is important for a composition that both shapes and residual shapes have interesting forms.

Fig. 99 Symmetry: Shapes from the Islamic motif of Fig. 80a were selected and placed so that, on both sides of the diagonal line, an identical figure developed.

Arranging: When using incidental patterns such as "scattered motifs," the arrangement in the design could be very chaotic. To obtain some harmony in the design, it is best to arrange motifs by using the same color or the same size (Fig. 100).

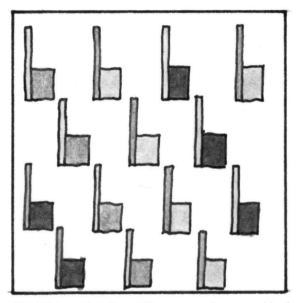

Fig. 100 Arranging: Two different rectangles are combined to form one motif, which has been applied repetitiously. A very strong composition developed from the way they are arranged, which is emphasized even more by the color choice.

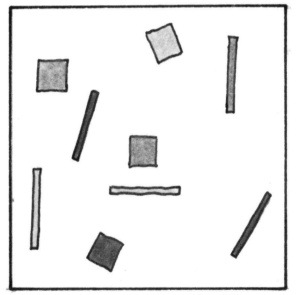

Fig. 101 The same rectangles are used here. They are not connected to each other, but used at irregular intervals. The result is a 'scattered motif.' Even the color choice is irregular.

58

Fig. 102 The swatches derived from the Islamic motif of Fig. 89 are all incorporated in this sweater. The elements of line, shape and color are worked in stockinette stitch, sometimes supported by purl stitches for a stronger effect. First the design was worked out on graph paper. Then a gauge swatch was knit in order to calculate how many stitches and rows are worked in one inch. Usually a stitch is less high than it is wide. When the design is worked out on squared graph paper, don't forget that the proportions of the design are somewhat distorted. The sweater is made in one piece so that the motif is not interrupted when going from the shoulders to the sleeves.

Fig. 103 Detail of Fig. 102.

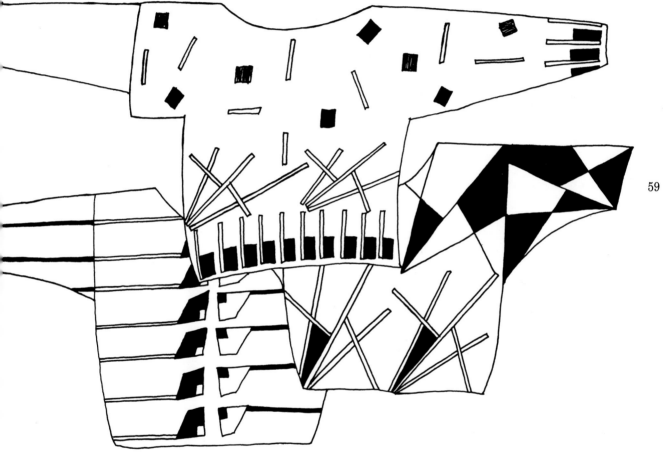

. 104 Sweaters designed on variations of the motif in Fig. 89.

5. THREE-DIMENSIONAL DESIGNING

In the preceding chapter we looked at knitted garments as being flat surfaces (two-dimensional). In many cases, a sweater consists of four pieces: front, back and two sleeves. By assembling these pieces, a three-dimensional form is developed that fits around the body. When you include straight lines in your design, you should be aware that on a flat surface they are indeed straight, but as soon as they are applied in clothing, the straight lines will look curved.

Sleeves can present another tricky problem. In designing a garment, one should pursue unity throughout. The sleeves, especially, can cause difficulties in achieving a balanced design.

Many times you see sweaters with beautiful designs on the front, while no attention has been given to the back or the sleeves. The easiest way to achieve unity would be to knit the sweater in one color, but that is, of course, not very original.

In this chapter we will pay special attention to the influence of three-dimensional designing on a composition. Some compositional difficulties can be prevented by using singular shapes instead of the traditional four pieces.

Singular shapes

Applying unusual fundamentals to your design can lead to very spectacular and original knits. Instead of taking the human body as a starting point, you could use abstract ideas.

Take for instance a square piece of fabric, with an opening cut in the middle for your head. This can give you all kinds of ideas to apply to your design. On this page we give you some examples. If you fold this cloth diagonally, you will get a totally different effect than when it is draped, so that the front and back form straight lines at the bottom. Several variations are possible: you could fold the corners back or let them overlap, you could connect the pieces or you could just let them hang loose (see also Fig. 13 and 17). You will probably come up with other variations yourself while designing, especially when you decide to use different colors in your design.

Sweaters with "bat wing" sleeves or a T-shaped sweater can be made in one piece. This can be done in two ways. You could start with the front, going over the shoulder to the back. The stitch pattern will be horizontal. But you could also start with one sleeve, making increases for the front and the back, and continue to the other sleeve. Then the stitch pattern is vertical. A vertical stripe in a design worked this way will technically be a lot easier, especially if you use several colors. The yarn only needs to be crossed at the beginning or at the end of the rows. The different effects of the direction of stitch patterns should be kept in mind when designing.

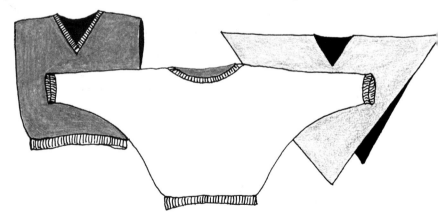

Fig. 105 The term "singular shape" means that the garment is made in one piece. The shape can be rectangular, square, circular, triangular or a fanciful round shape, as in a "bat wing" sweater. The sweaters shown are all worked in one piece. The one on the left has a rectangular shape with an opening for the head to go through, the middle one is rather cross-shaped with round corners and the one on the right has a square shape, diagonally folded.

Fig. 106 In knitted garments it is possible to form shapes whose appearances form a direct link with the way they were constructed. In this example, for instance, the circle could well be used as the basis for a garment. The circle is made by knitting in short rows. When 50 sts are cast on, you only work 10 sts in the first row. Turn the work and work back over these 10 sts, slipping the first st after turning. On the next row you knit 20 sts, turn the work, and work back again. Continue this sequence with 30 and 40 sts and finally the last row over 50 sts. A segment of a circle is created this way. By repeating this working method, a full circle will be developed. The width of the circle can be varied by adding one or more extra rows, in which all stitches are knit at the same time. An extra effect can be achieved if different colors are used.

Composite shapes

A sweater can be knit in several ways; in one piece, like the sweater with "bat wing" sleeves or in several pieces, like a sweater with raglan sleeves. A sweater with raglan or regular sleeves normally consists of four pieces: front, back and two sleeves. It is also possible to knit a sweater in more than four pieces, where the pieces are either knitted together or sewn together by hand. The shape of the sweater depends on the design. If your design calls for a horizontal bar that continues on the sleeves, it will be much better to knit the sweater in one piece so the bar is uninterrupted.

The sweater shown on page 63 is composed of several pieces. On all sides of the triangles, stitches are picked up to form new triangles. A description of this sweater is given in Fig. 108.

In following such a procedure, the starting point is a repeated use of one shape (in this case a triangle) from which a three-dimensional form, a sweater, is created. The sleeves, as well as the back and front, form a unity, despite the fact that it is composed of a considerable number of small pieces.

There is a fundamental difference between this approach and the one in which a flat surface (the front of the sweater) is filled in with triangular motifs (two-dimensional designing).

62

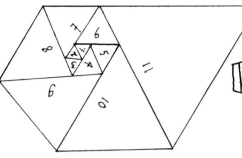

Fig. 108 Sweater with triangles.
This sweater is worked as follows:
The base of one triangle is knit with 5 stitches. On the right edge of the triangle, stitches are bound off at each edge until there is 1 st left on the needle. Bind off. On one side of the triangle, the same amount of sts are picked up and used for the base of the triangle, which is 5 sts wide. This will be the base for the second triangle. Bind off the sts as before, until there is one st left. Bind off this st. At the edge of this 2nd triangle a third triangle is made. Now pick up 10 sts along the edges of triangles 1 and 3 (see drawing), which will be the base for the 4th triangle.
For the fifth triangle stitches are picked up at the side of triangle 4. The base of triangle 6 consists of 15 sts, as the stitches are picked up to form triangles 5 and 1. In this way the triangles are getting bigger.

Fig. 109 To obtain the shape of a sweater, make a paper pattern of the correct size, then place the knitted piece on it, to see whether it is big enough. Parts of the piece can also be folded over the shoulders to form part of the back. Of course, it is not possible to compose the whole sweater like this. Sometimes loose triangles must be knit, which are sewn on by hand. It is advisable to make triangles with a multiple of 5 sts for the base. Otherwise you will not be able to sew the pieces together. At the end of the sleeves a border was knit in ribbing. The collar and bottom edges are also finished in ribbing.

Fig. 107 If a sweater is built up out of loose sections, that can be emphasized by knitting these sections in different colors.

Fig. 110 Front. The sweater is made of a thick cotton with size 6 needles in stockinette stitch. The colors are bright and are worked in such a way that the sides of triangles of the same color do not touch each other.

Fig. 110a Back of the sweater shown in Fig. 110.

Sweater with horizontal and vertical strips

A sweater can also be composed of strips. This method was applied in the sweater with color blends in Fig. 111. When using many different colors, it is easier to knit the strips separately. The effect is even more striking when you use solid colors for each strip. Besides sewing the strips together, you could also weave them horizontally or vertically.

Garment composed of five triangles

The best way to come up with original sweater shapes would be to take a piece of paper and cut out different shapes and play with them. That's the way the sweater in Fig. 112 developed, which is composed of five triangles (without a corner). When you use a soft and smooth yarn, the sweater will fit nicely and feel very comfortable.

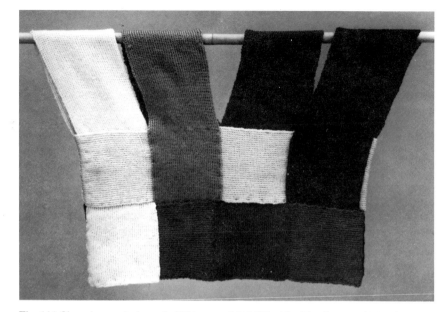

Fig. 111 Six strips are knit, each 48″ long and 5-1/4″ wide. The four vertical strips go from white to black. The horizontal strips are pink and purple.

Form and composition

Form

The specific form of a garment is definitely linked to the one who wears it. The sweater is a "three-dimensional substance" in which the body is the "supporting frame." Picture a sweater, for instance, as being a statue. You will be able to see all sides from different angles. This is very important to remember when making a composition. Do not think only of the decorations on the front of the sweater, but keep in mind that the composition should form an entity throughout.

It does not matter where the composition is begun, at the sleeve or at a specific side of the sweater, as long as the rest of the design conforms.

With three-dimensional designing you have the opportunity to follow the natural shapes, like the ones applied in Greek sculptures. Used in clothing, this will lead to comfortable garments in which parts of the human body, like shoulders, waist, arms and bust, are taken into account.

Another possibility is to accentuate specific parts, sometimes determined by the current fashion; for example, the oversized shoulders, or a slim waistline.

On the other hand, you can conceal certain body parts. Think of existing cultures where a woman is not allowed to show certain parts of her body. Shawls and capes are used to keep the body warm, but also to conceal what's underneath. In a cape, even the arms are disregarded since there are no sleeves in it. The fashion of oversized clothing is another example of concealing body parts.

When taking into consideration that you have the opportunity to accentuate or to conceal parts of the body, you will discover new forms.

Fig. 112 A garment composed of five triangles of the same size (see also Fig. 113).

Composition

In general, there is not much difference between two- and three-dimensional designing, except for the spatial aspect of the latter.

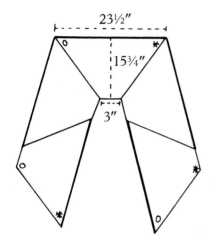

Line

In hand-knitting, lines can be formed by knitting rows in another color, or in a different material. These lines lie horizontally across the knitwear. You could also form vertical or diagonal lines.

In order to determine the specific position of lines, make sure that the unity is not disturbed. For instance, a diagonal line carried over the shoulders, or a horizontal line on the sleeves or on front and back can have a very special effect.

Seen in the whole composition, the sleeves create a distinctive problem. As a body moves, the form of a garment changes as well. Take for example a T-shaped sweater, on which uninterrupted horizontal lines are going from one sleeve, across the front, to the other sleeve. In order to see this design clearly, you should spread your arms.

If you keep your arms down or put them high up, however, the lines will produce a completely different effect.

Fig. 113 The garment on page 65 consists of five triangles. The bases of the triangles (in the drawing these lines are bold) are 24″ wide. Every 2nd row bind off 1 stitch at each edge. When the remaining width is about 3-1/2″, bind off all stitches. The height of each triangle will be about 16″. This garment is made on a knitting machine. To prevent the edges from rolling, you could work the first inch of the triangles in ribbing, so that the back, the sleeves and the front neckline have borders. To get borders at the bottom of the front sections and the back part of the neckline, stitches are picked up from the triangles and worked in ribbing. The X and O markings indicate how pieces are put together. The front sections can also hang loose or be fastened. When the borders of the triangles are worked in the picot edge instead of ribbing, the borders will roll as in the example in Fig. 112.

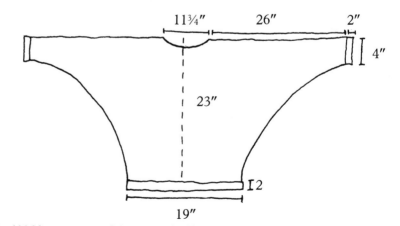

Fig. 114 Measurements of the sweater in Fig. 115.

Fig. 115 This red/pink sweater with black stripes is made in one piece, beginning at one sleeve. The red bands are 4″ and the pink ones 6″ wide. Four black stripes interrupt the band pattern in red and pink. They are knit in diagonally and continue over the shoulders.

Shapes and form

When using forms, different colors or stitches, basically the same thing is happening. A big triangle on the sleeve will look curved, because sweaters have a tendency to follow the curves of the body.

Another aspect that should be taken into account is the relationship between the three-dimensional form of the sweater and the two-dimensional forms on the surface. For instance, if you design a sweater in a rectangular form (three-dimensional), the same rectangle can be repeated on the flat surface (two-dimensional) in colors and stitches. A very close harmony is achieved. If you are looking for contrasts, however, you could fill in the rectangle on the flat surface with round and fanciful forms.

68

Fig. 116 The shape of this sweater is based on a triangle. In this design the shape is repeated and distorted at the same time by overlapping it by a fanciful shape.

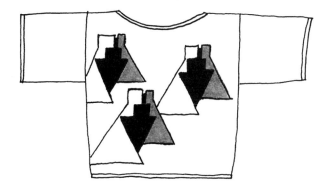

Fig. 117 This design shows triangles that overlap each other. An arrow in a contrasting color is placed on top of the triangles. The sweater itself is composed of simple rectangles.

Fig. 118 This jacket consists of loose triangles that overlapp each other. In the design, the same overlapping triangles are found in back.

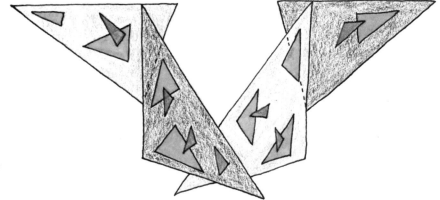

Overlapping

Even overlapping can create designs in which two-dimensional forms harmonize with the three-dimensional form of the sweater. In Fig. 118 a pattern of two triangles overlapping each other is applied to a garment. The front of this jacket consists of two similar triangular shaped pieces of fabric which overlap each other when closing the garment—a good example of combining two- and three-dimensional designs in one project.

Size

In the design of Fig. 118, another principle is applied by varying the size of forms in a repetitiously used pattern. The triangles used for the closure of the jacket are much larger than the ones used in the pattern throughout the garment.

Contrasts

Contrasts are very often used in sweater designs. For example, colors are used to create a contrast between the front and the back of the sweater. You could also work the left front in a different color than the right front. Sometimes contrasts can be interrupted by intentionally using the original background color. Ribbing and collars are also very suitable to knit in contrasting colors. Using contrasting materials can make a dull design very exciting. Diagonal stripes on a sweater, worked in a glossy cotton on a background of regular matte cotton, will give a totally different look. You can also make contrasts in shapes. A big flower design on a

square-shaped sweater is quite possible. To maintain unity, you could incorporate the square shape of the sweater in the design by placing the flower motifs on a background of square shapes, for example.

Symbols

In some cases contrasts can have a symbolic value. Contrasts in shapes and colors can symbolize the difference between light and dark, male and female, etc. At the same time these contrasting shapes and colors, when used together, can form a unity.

69

Texture (materials and stitches)

The way a sweater is constructed mainly determines the shape it will take when it is worn. Since knits are stretchable, it is very easy to obtasin a very flexible piece of fabric that shapes comfortably around the body. Some materials are more flexible than others. A soft thin wool shapes easier than rope, for instance. You can also change the texture of knits by using different stitches. The characteristics of different stitch patterns can be used when, for example, you would like to stiffen (strengthen) certain parts or make them more flexible. If you want to knit oversized shoulders, you should knit these in a stiffer material, using a stitch pattern that has the same effect.

On other parts, more flexible material is better. In that case, flexible stitches, like the fisherman stitch and ribbing are used. Ribbing is extremely supple and is used for borders, collars and waists.

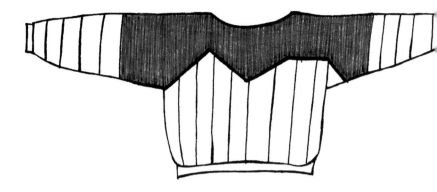

Fig. 119 This sweater is made in one piece, begun at one sleeve end. The shoulder section is worked by adding a thin yarn of a different color at the indicated places. This way the shoulder section is accentuated.

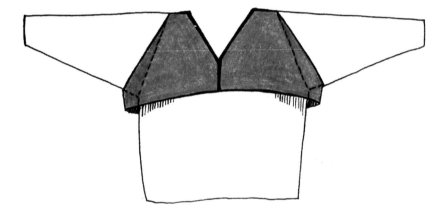

Fig. 120 In order to reinforce the shoulder, separate shoulder sections are knit in a sturdier material than the rest of the sweater.

6. TECHNICAL ASPECTS

Calculating the pattern.

In order to be able to calculate the pattern, you need to have the measurements of hips, waist, wrist, length of back, width of shoulder, neck, chest, sleeve at underarm and length of sleeves (see Fig. 121). You could also take these measurements from an existing sweater. Draw the design on paper and fill in the measurements.

The stitches and needles to be used should be calculated on the basis of these measurements. This is done by knitting a tension or gauge swatch. Work a square slightly larger than 4″ in the stitch pattern you have chosen for the sweater. Place the swatch on a flat surface by using pins. Count the rows and stitches between the pins.

In Fig. 122, 4″ is 20 stitches and 25 rows. When the hips measure 32″, the stitches to be cast on for the front of the sweater (16″ wide) should be: 4 x 20 equals 80 stitches. This is the same for the back.

The length of the sweater should be 20″, as 25 rows measured 4″, and the length should be 20″, so 125 rows should be knitted (5 x 25 = 125).

This way you can calculate the entire sweater.

Diagonal lines as used for a V-neckline or a raglan sleeve, can be calculated as follows.

In Fig. 116 a V-neckline is drawn which is 50 rows deep and 15 stitches wide. These 15 sts should be evenly decreased over 50 rows to form the V-line. By binding off 1 st every 3 rows, 15 sts will be decreased over a total of 45 rows. Work 5 more rows on the shoulder side in order to get 50 rows.

For the sleeves, increases are made the same way. For example: cast on 36 sts. After the ribbing, 4 sts are increased evenly spaced across the first row. As the upper sleeve should be 80 sts wide, 40 sts need to be increased. The length of the sleeve is 100 rows. As the increases are made at each edge (one at the beginning and one at the end equals 2 sts per row), you need 20 rows to increase 40 stitches. On a total of 100 rows, this means that you need to make the increases every fifth row.

Ribbing is usually knit on smaller size needles than the rest of the sweater, in order to let it fit tightly around the hips or waist. To obtain a bloused effect, stitches are increased across the first row of the stitch pattern or the last row of ribbing.

The length of the back is measured from neck to waist, although sweaters are usually made a little longer. The drawing in Fig. 121 is very much simplified and is not a standard size.

Estimating yarn quantities

Usually wool labels indicate how much yarn is in a skein. It is

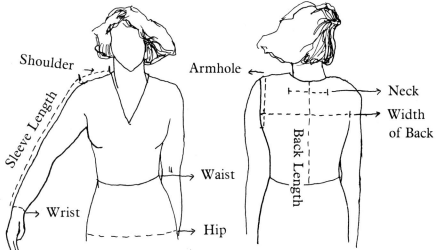

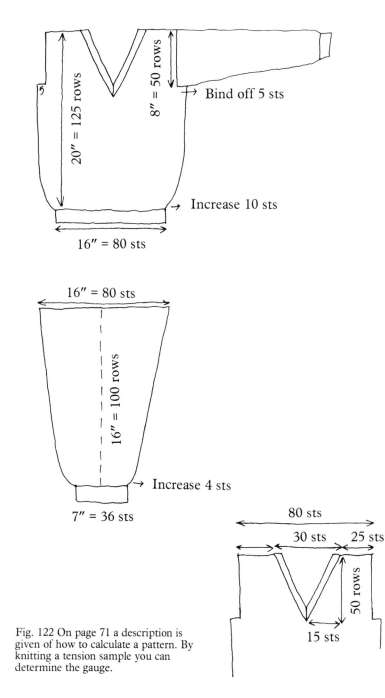

20" = 125 rows

8" = 50 rows

Bind off 5 sts

Increase 10 sts

16" = 80 sts

16" = 80 sts

16" = 100 rows

Increase 4 sts

7" = 36 sts

80 sts

30 sts 25 sts

50 rows

15 sts

Fig. 122 On page 71 a description is given of how to calculate a pattern. By knitting a tension sample you can determine the gauge.

advised to buy a little extra yarn when you start a knitting project, and make sure they have the same dyelot number. Balls that are not used can often be returned to the store where you bought the yarn. It is not easy to give a general rule here to determine how much yarn you need. There are several factors involved: the size needles, the thickness of the yarn, the measure of elasticity of the garment, the way you knit and the stitches you use.

The finishing touch
When you design clothing, you should realize that besides the large pieces it is composed of, the smaller details are just as important.
First of all, the joining of the pieces by seams: they are normally hand or machine sewn, in an almost invisible way. By using a special selvage stitch (sl first st at each row purlwise), an invisible seam can be produced. On the other hand, it can be very interesting to emphasize these parts of a garment.
In sweaters with raglan sleeves, this is done by decreasing the stitches as follows. At the beginning of a row: 1 selv. st sl 1 Kwise and K the next stitch, pass the sl st over the K1, and at the end of the row: K 2 tog, 1 selv st.
The diagonal line of the sleeve is accentuated this way. An even stronger emphasis can be obtained by knitting an eyelet or openwork pattern, or knitting the line in a different color.
Borders on sleeves, neck and bottom edges are usually knit in the same color as the rest of the sweater and are worked in ribbing because of its

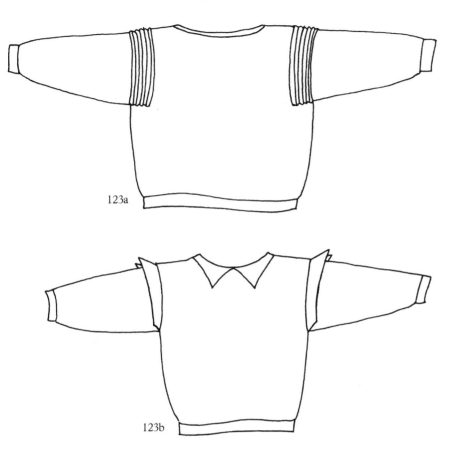

123a

123b

Fig. 123a Where the sleeves meet the front and back, the seams are accentuated by knitting the last rows of the sleeves in a different stitch, such as ribbing.

Fig. 123b In this sweater the sleeves are also accentuated. Extra pieces are knitted on front and back, while the sleeves go underneath these flaps.

Fig. 123c Front and back are composed of different colored strips. The seams that are used to join the several strips can be emphasized by using a thicker yarn in a different color.

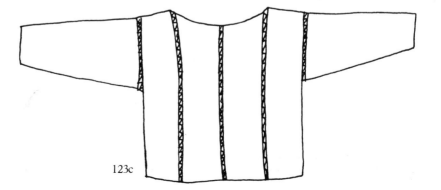

123c

elastic characteristic. If you decide not to work in ribbing, it is recommended that elastic thread be knitted in at the hems.

On the other hand, you are free to choose borders that hang loose instead of the tight-fitting borders in ribbing. Again that depends on the current fashion and what you like.

In the past, sweaters were made to keep warm and ribbed borders were a necessity.

If you, for instance, design a sweater with straight lines, the use of ribbing can distort the effect of the lines, because the elasticity of the ribbing will make the lines look curved. For a different finish here, you may choose, for instance, a stockinette stitch hem. This is worked as follows. First knit the desired depth of the hem in St st, then knit one row on the wrong (purl) side, to mark the folding edge of the hem. Continue by working the same number of rows in St st as you knitted before the folding edge. Fold the hem to the back and catch the cast-on edge in the next row of knitting. Insert the needle through both stitches that lie on top of each other and knit them together.

Sleeves

The shape of the sleeves should form a unity with the rest of the sweater. If the front and back of the sweater have a rectangular shape, you can use the same shape for the sleeves. As the width of the sleeves at the shoulders is different from the width at the wrists, you have to decrease stitches when you start with the shoulders and increase

stitches when you start with the wrists. T-shaped sweaters are usually made in one piece. At the underarm of the sleeves, stitches are increased. For straight lined sleeves, you could increase all stitches at once on both sides of the sweater. In most cases it is best to increase the stitches over several rows. Of course this depends on the style of your sweater. You will have many stitches on the needles when both sleeves and front are worked on at the same time. But as soon as you shape the

neckline, you can divide the work into two equal parts and work each side separately. The advantage of knitting a sweater in one piece is that motifs that are designed to go from front to sleeves are not interrupted by seams.

In "bat wing" shaped sweaters, the increases are made gradually, starting right above the ribbing. Eventually, there are enough stitches on the needle to form the sleeves. How many stitches need to be increased each row depends on the

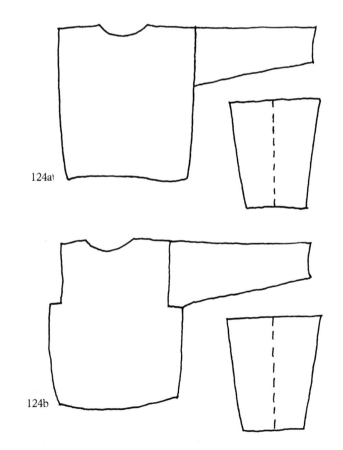

124a

124b

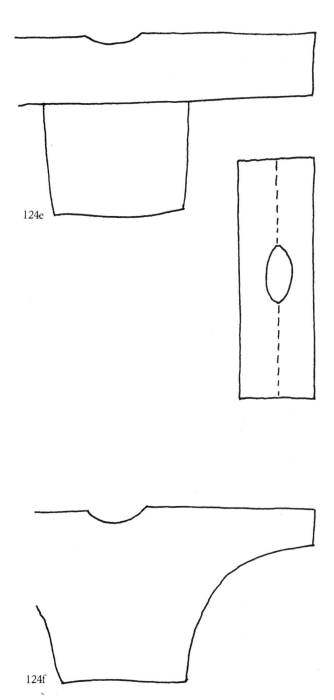

124e

124f

75

Fig. 124 Various sleeve types:
a. Dropped shoulder. The edges of front and back are in a straight line, with no shaping.
b. Peasant sleeve. In front and back, armholes are shaped by binding off a number of stitches at the same time. The sleeves should be a little longer than the dropped shoulder sleeve.
c. Set-in sleeve.
d. Raglan sleeve.
e. Sleeves knit in one piece.
f. "Bat wing" sleeve.

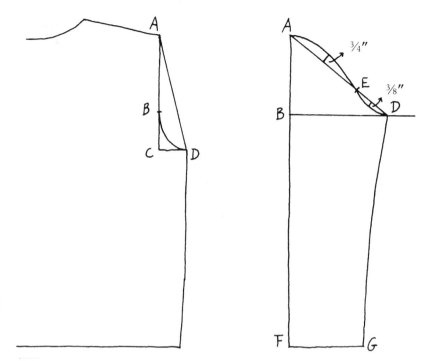

Fig. 125 A pattern for a set-in sleeve is drawn as follows.
A-C = depth of armhole
A-F = sleeve length
A-B = two thirds of depth of armhole.
Draw a horizontal line from left to right at B and F. On the front, measure the distance between A and D. Add 1-1/4″ and mark it out on the sleeve, as shown.
D-E = a third of D-A
F-G = half of wrist width + 1-1/4″ or more, depending on the width you choose.
Draw the rounding of the sleeve top and measure to see if it fits in the armhole. The sleeve may be slightly bigger.
You can now transfer the sleeve pattern to paper. In order to find out how many stitches should be bound off for the sleeve top, it may be a good idea to place the paper pattern on the already finished front or back, and count the stitches to be decreased.
The decreases for the armholes in front and back should form a smooth line as well. If you take the example of Fig. 118, where 4″ = 20 stitches, and you would like to have an armhole with a depth of 2″ (= 10 stitches), you could bind off the stitches as follows: 3 sts 1 time, 2 sts 2 times, 1 st 3 times.

style of the sweater and the thickness of the yarn. It is important to space the increases evenly, for instance, one stitch per row, to obtain a smooth line.
By making a gauge swatch it is easy to find out how many stitches need to be increased in every row.

Necklines and collars
Necklines and collars are very important features of clothing. They can be decorative, and they are used as finishes.
A collar can either be knit in the same material and stitch pattern as the sweater, or it can be varied.
a. The boat-neck is one of the easiest necklines. Back and front of the sweater are worked until a certain length, and all stitches are bound off at the same time (usually after a few rows of ribbing as finishing). Then the shoulder seams can be joined.
b. Another possibility is a round neckline. To knit a round neckline, the stitches of the front of a sweater should be divided into 3 equal parts. If you have 90 sts, the division will be: 30-30-30.
Each shoulder now consists of 30 stitches. To form the round neckline, the 30 center stitches are not bound off at the same time. At about 2″ from the shoulder, stitches are gradually bound off. For example: bind off 14 sts at one time (center sts). Then on both sides of the neckline (each part is worked individually), on every 2nd or right side of work, bind off 3 sts, 2 sts, 2 sts and 1 st.
c. A traditional V-neckline starts a little bit above the underarm. In order to get a smooth neckline, we

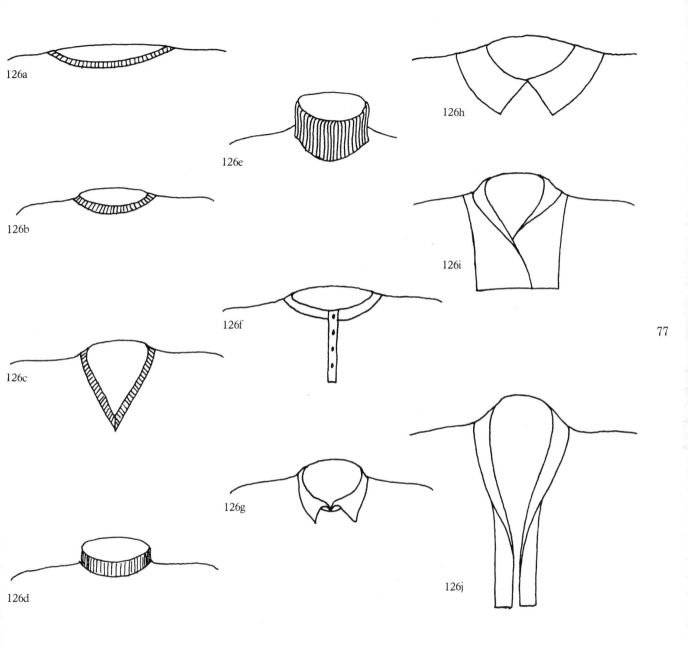

126a

126b

126c

126d

126e

126f

126g

126h

126i

126j

Fig. 126 Various necklines and collars:
a. boat-neck, b. round neckline, c. V-neckline, d. stand-up collar, e. turtleneck, f. polo-neck, g. flat collar, h. flat wide collar, i. and j. shawl collar.

Fig. 127 V-neckline
Divide the front into two equal parts.
Right front: Knit across row until there are 4 sts left. Then: K2, pass the 1st K st over the 2nd, K1, selv st.
Left front: Right side of work: selv st, K1, K2 tog, work to end of row.
Border: Pick up all stitches along neckline.
Do not pick up the selvage stitches.

g. A stand-up collar can turn into a flat collar when a slit is made in the front.

h. For a flat round collar it is necessary to evenly increase stitches across the shoulder and the back.

i. For the short shawl collar, first you knit a square neckline. Pick up the stitches on the back and sides of the neckline and work in ribbing until you reach the exact width. Bind off all stitches. At the center front, the left and right parts of the collar are fastened (overlapped).

j. For a shawl collar for a vest, a deep V-shape is necessary. Along both fronts and the neck, stitches are taken up and worked in ribbing, without making any decreases. All the abovementioned collars are symmetrical.

would like to refer to the procedure described in Fig. 127. To carry out the decreases, the work is divided into two equal parts. This type of neckline is extremely suitable when using triangular shapes in your design. It can be applied to the front as well as the back of the sweater. The depth of the V, of course, can be varied.

d. A stand-up collar can be made by picking up stitches from the neck and working in ribbing for 2 1/2″.

Interfacing may be used for stiffening the collar.

e. The stand-up collar can be made longer to form a turtleneck. If you make the round neck a little wide, the turtleneck will consequently get wider as well.

f. For the polo-neck, the work is divided into two equal parts. On both sides extra stitches should be cast on (for example 3). These 6 stitches are worked in ribbing, in which button holes can be made.

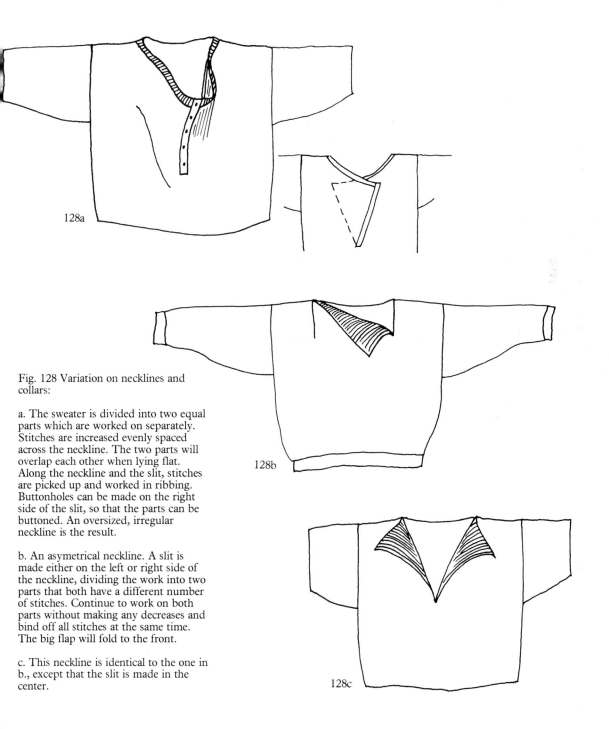

Fig. 128 Variation on necklines and collars:

a. The sweater is divided into two equal parts which are worked on separately. Stitches are increased evenly spaced across the neckline. The two parts will overlap each other when lying flat. Along the neckline and the slit, stitches are picked up and worked in ribbing. Buttonholes can be made on the right side of the slit, so that the parts can be buttoned. An oversized, irregular neckline is the result.

b. An asymetrical neckline. A slit is made either on the left or right side of the neckline, dividing the work into two parts that both have a different number of stitches. Continue to work on both parts without making any decreases and bind off all stitches at the same time. The big flap will fold to the front.

c. This neckline is identical to the one in b., except that the slit is made in the center.

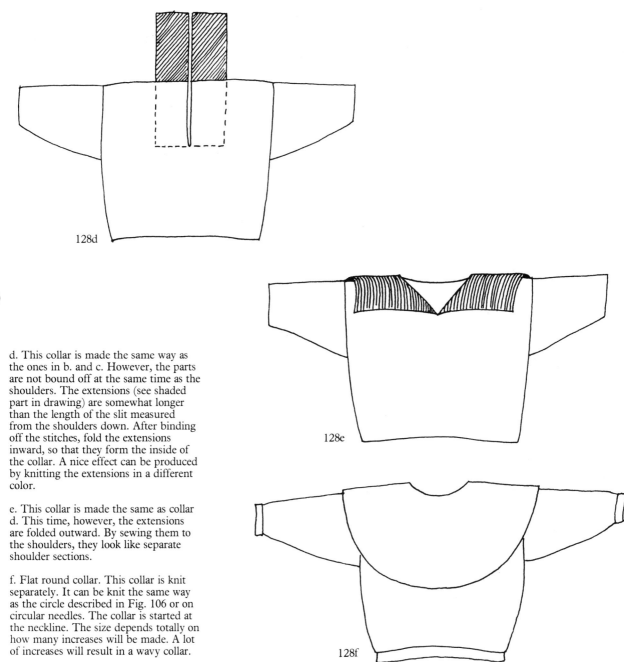

128d

d. This collar is made the same way as the ones in b. and c. However, the parts are not bound off at the same time as the shoulders. The extensions (see shaded part in drawing) are somewhat longer than the length of the slit measured from the shoulders down. After binding off the stitches, fold the extensions inward, so that they form the inside of the collar. A nice effect can be produced by knitting the extensions in a different color.

e. This collar is made the same as collar d. This time, however, the extensions are folded outward. By sewing them to the shoulders, they look like separate shoulder sections.

f. Flat round collar. This collar is knit separately. It can be knit the same way as the circle described in Fig. 106 or on circular needles. The collar is started at the neckline. The size depends totally on how many increases will be made. A lot of increases will result in a wavy collar.

128e

128f

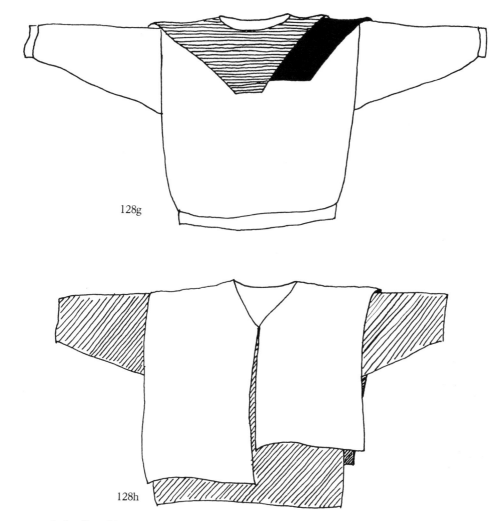

128g

128h

g. A flat asymmetrical collar with square edges. For this collar, cast on the required number of stitches and make increases at both edges. The increases to be made are different for each side. On the left side increase stitches every 2nd row and on the right side every 4th row. Shape neckline as front and back.

h. Here the collar consists of long straight flaps that almost cover the whole sweater.

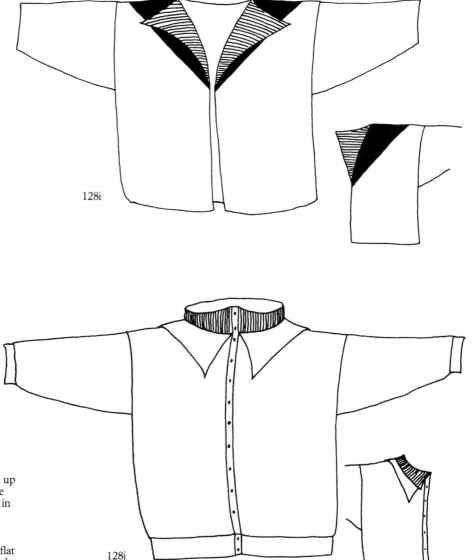

128i

82

i. For this collar, stitches are picked up from the neckline and worked in the same triangle shape as already used in the design of the sweater. When finished, the collar is folded back.

j. Stand-up collar combined with a flat collar. The buttonhole border from the front is continued in the stand-up collar, so that the collar can be closed. In this design a flat collar is used as well. Notice that the front of the stand-up collar is a little longer than the back. When unbuttoned and folded back, it will lie on top of the flat collar.

128j

k. A scarf is knitted separately. You could do that by making a neckline as shown in example b. The stitches for the scarf are picked up from the side of the flap and worked until you reach the desired length.

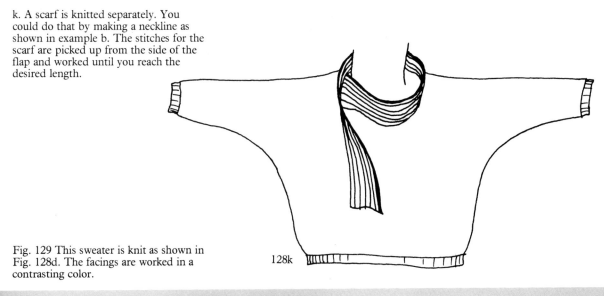

128k

Fig. 129 This sweater is knit as shown in Fig. 128d. The facings are worked in a contrasting color.

Closures

Knitted garments normally do not need closures because of their flexibility. Children's knitwear often has closures at the neck side (see Fig. 76). Some closures are worked in such a way that, for instance, front and back are partially overlapping each other, so that no buttons or snaps are needed.

In some clothing where closures are used, as in vests or jackets, it is recommended that the shape of the closures be adapted to the shape of the garment.

Closures can also become an extra feature of the garment. Triangular buttons in a triangular-shaped sweater form a stronger whole. Sometimes a closure is necessary.

An inconspicuous or blind closure can be made by knitting an overlap and a facing, behind which the closure (for example, hooks and eyes, snaps, velcro or buttons and buttonholes) are hidden.

Sometimes closures are so original that they can be used as decorations. Experimenting with non-traditional closures can be very exciting.

You could, for instance, knit a slit in one side of a garment, by which the flap of the other side can be pulled through (Fig. 130). Or you could tie the flaps in a knot, so that the width can be varied. With fabric remnants you can explore which application will be best for your design.

84

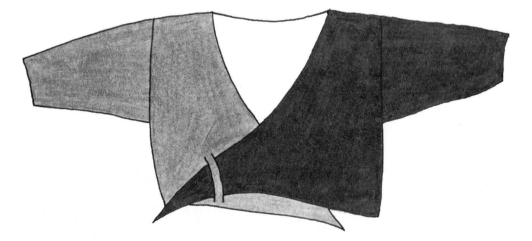

Fig. 130 This vest can be closed by pulling the left front flap through the two slits made in the right front flap.

Buttonholes

A buttonhole is really nothing more than a slit in a garment. A horizontal buttonhole is made by binding off a number of stitches. To determine the width of the buttonhole, place the button on the knitted piece and count the stitches covered by its diameter.

Cast the stitches on again over the bound off sts in the next row.

To make a vertical buttonhole, each side is worked separately. At the base of the slit, join a second ball of yarn. Knit the required number of rows. Join both halves by working across both sets of stitches with one ball of yarn again.

A nice way to finish the buttonholes is to work the stitches around it in ribbing. You could also finish the buttonhole by hand with the buttonhole stitch or crochet around the buttonhole.

Tiny buttonholes, used for baby clothes, are made in the eyelet pattern: on the right side of work, yo, K2 tog. Purling the next row will result in a small hole, where the yarn-over was used.

131a

131b

Fig. 131 Pockets
a. Sewn-on pocket.
b. Knit-in pocket.
c. The front consists of four parts. The two bottom parts are rectangular and are worked in double knit to form pockets.
d. Pockets knitted separately and sewn on by hand.
e. Pockets with a triangular shaped border. The borders can hang loose or be attached by a button.
f. Pockets that echo the shapes in the design of the sweater.

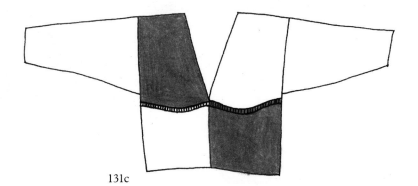

131c

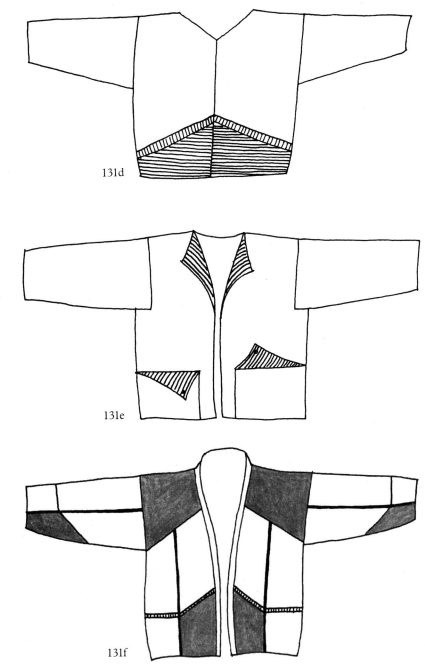

131d

86

131e

131f

Pockets

We already mentioned several times in this book that it is very important that certain details of clothing should be in conformity with the total shape of the garment. Too many times a pocket seems to have the same "old" triangular shape that is placed as inconspicuously as possible somewhere on the sweater. But a pocket can definitely be a decoration and form an essential part of the sweater. A simple sweater design worked in stockinette stitch in one color can be brightened up by knitting the pockets and borders in a contrasting color. And as far as the shape of a pocket is concerned, why not use a circular or other fanciful shape instead. Especially in clothing, where sewn and knitted parts are combined, there are numerous possibilities. There are three ways to knit a pocket:

1. By knitting a separate piece in a certain shape and attaching it to the sweater. It should be pointed out though that it is very important that the knitted shape has nicely finished edges. Here you can choose out of the many existing varieties of selvage stitches.

Or you could knit the borders of the pocket in ribbing (in the same or different color). The pocket can be sewn "invisibly" to the garment by applique, using a slip stitch, or by a decorative topstitch ina contrasting color. When you choose the latter option, use a color that will be repeated somewhere else in the sweater to obtain unity in the design.

2. There is also an "invisible" way of knitting-in the pockets at the same time. Knit the part of the sweater where you want to incorporate the pocket until you reach the edge for the borders. Knit a few rows in ribbing across the determined width of the pockets and bind off the stitches.

On separate needles knit a separate piece on the same number of stitches that you just bound off. This piece will be the pocket lining. When you reach the required length, the stitches can be placed on the regular needles again where they replace the stitches that were bound off earlier. The loose hanging pocket should be sewn to the inside of the garment.

3. A third way to make a pocket is to work in double knit. At the place where the pocket should be, pick up twice as many stitches as required for the finished pocket. Two layers are knit at the same time (see also directions given on page 47). It is important that at the sides of the pockets the threads are crossed properly, so that the pocket will be completely attached to the garment. When the pocket is finished, bind off the extra stitches and continue the rest of the garment.

7. COMBINING KNITS WITH WOVEN FABRIC

Combining knitted pieces with woven fabric increases the design possibilities of clothing.

As a starting point for designing this way, you could take examples from your daily environment or you could use the already existing woven fabrics and start from there.

In the figure shown on this page, an example is shown of a piece of fabric in houndstooth check. On it, separate knitted pieces are placed, worked in different stitches based on the design of the fabric.

They are either knit in the same color or in the same design. In Fig. 133 you can see where the fabric and the knitted pieces are used in the design.

Fig. 132 Fabric in the houndstooth check variation in green, white and dark blue was taken as the starting point for a design. The separate knitted pieces placed on the fabric are knit either in the same color or in the same design as the fabric.
a. An imitation of the houndstooth check, in which the check is a little bigger.
b. A Stockinette stitch swatch, in which light and dark green stitches are alternated.
c. Fisherman stitch in two colors (see page 38).

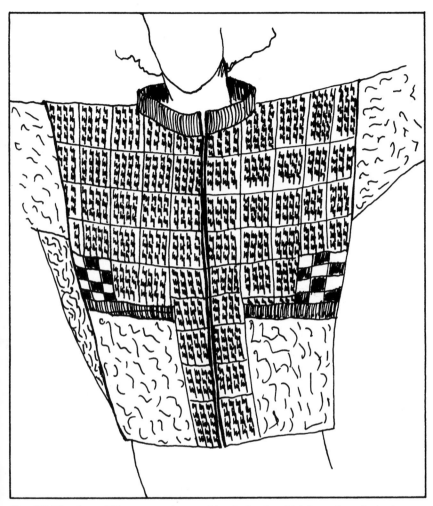

Fig. 133 The three different swatches used in a jacket in which houndstooth check fabric forms the background.

Fig. 134 Another way of combining fabric and knitted pieces.

WITH THANKS TO

Els Mulder, Simone Klaasen, Jola van de Wateren, Carla Selhorst, Marjan Groot, Elly Pleiter, Wytske Osinga-Zuiderdorp, J. Pleiter-Dijk, M.C. Bredewold-Severijn, Gerda Brinkman.

The yarns used in this book are from Scheepjeswool.

Superwash Zermatt: sweater with zebra design, Fig. 12
Mayflower: sweater in two colors, Fig. 17; sweater, Fig. 129
Granada: baby sweater with cables, Fig. 67; baby sweater, Fig. 76; sweater based on an Islamic motif, Fig. 102
Cotton Satin: sweater in fisherman stitch, Fig. 63
Invicta Extra: sweater based on Picasso painting, Fig. 49; sweater with embroidered motifs, Fig. 54
Superwash Cable: sweater composed of strips, Fig. 111; sweater composed of five triangles, Fig. 112
Linnen: sweater in open work pattern, Fig. 60

INDEX

92